Writing the Revolution

Cultural Criticism from
Left Review

Edited by DAVID MARGOLIES

 Pluto  Press

LONDON · CHICAGO, ILLINOIS

First published 1998 by Pluto Press
345 Archway Road, London N6 5AA
and 1436 West Randolph, Chicago, Illinois 60607, USA

British Library Cataloguing in Publication Data
A catalogue record for this book is available from
the British Library

ISBN 0 7453 1161 X hbk

Library of Congress Cataloging in Publication Data
Writing the revolution : cultural criticism from Left review / edited
  by David Margolies
      p.   cm.
   Includes bibliographical references (p.   ) and index.
    ISBN 0–7453–1161–X
    1. Literature, Modern—20th century—History and criticism.
  I. Margolies, David. II. Left review (London, England)
  PN771.W74   1994
  801'.95'094109043—dc21   97–23977
                                                        CIP

Designed and produced for Pluto Press by
Chase Production Services, Chadlington, OX7 3LN
Printed in the EC

Contents

Acknowledgements

I would like to express my thanks to Lawrence and Wishart for their cooperation in this project, and also to Frank Cass Publishers. The staff of Marx Memorial Library were very helpful, and I am grateful to Andy Croft and Noreen Branson for assistance on specific points. I especially want to thank Nick Jacobs for his generous encouragement, advice and help. Finally, I am grateful to Sandra Margolies for her good-natured tolerance of my obsession with *Left Review*.

A Note on the Treatment and Order of Texts

I have usually reproduced original spelling and punctuation, despite its inconsistency, but have silently corrected obvious typographical errors. *Left Review*'s editors were not particularly concerned about consistency – they did not attempt to regularise ise/ize, or where punctuation falls in relation to a final quotation mark, but allowed the authors their own preferences, which I have not altered. Punctuation, similarly, is at best erratic, but I have not sought to change it. The speed of production, the political-practical demands, the direction of attention to other matters meant that many details escaped editorial attention; on balance, it was worth it.

The writing in *Left Review*, like most things written as long ago as the 1930s, exhibits the linguistic deficiencies of the age in regard to gender: it uses a non-inclusive language. I have not thought it otherwise useful to draw attention to it.

At the beginning of each selection I have given the month and year of publication, at the end the numbers and the pages from which it was taken. In the introductory comments I have given volume, issue number and pages in parentheses. Numbered notes in the extracts are the authors'; mine are indicated by an asterisk.

The selections have been organised into five sections. The first – The Writers' International Controversy – contains selections from the argument sustained over four issues about the nature of literature and art and how they should be employed now.

The second section is selections on the nature of literature and art. These are theoretical contributions but, unlike academic theory, they are not always obviously theoretical; sometimes they are only incidentally so, having been written for a slightly different purpose, and they generally avoid a theoretical vocabulary.

Cultural Critique, the third section, has selections dealing with the character of culture as a whole. The pieces concern aspects of the relation between social organisation and culture and the ideological functioning of culture.

The fourth section is composed of pieces relating to critical method and specific studies. It includes concrete examinations of works or genres, embodying the principles enunciated in Section II but not so much articulating them.

Finally, the fifth section, on readers' competitions, contains a few selections of material addressed to would-be competitors and also raises questions that are fundamental to the democratic functioning of culture.

Introduction

Left Review was a brilliant moment in left literary criticism and cultural democracy. In the three and a half years of its existence, October 1934 to May 1938, it produced the first Marxist literary theory in Britain and a body of criticism of striking originality. It was born of the spirit of the Popular Front – or People's Front, as it was known in Britain – which had been organised to stop fascism and whose policy, as the name suggests, was based on reaching out to people who shared the concern about social injustice and threats to democracy. As Harry Pollitt, leader of the Communist Party, put it in a *Left Review* editorial, 'We express our readiness to work with anyone and everyone who is opposed to the National Government and its policy of support for Fascism abroad and reaction at home' (II, 15: 799). The People's Front was indeed successful in drawing support from people outside the traditional left and even from some Conservatives, and *Left Review* had a welcoming attitude toward its readers regardless of their background. A wide range of people prominent in arts and letters, at that time or later, appeared in its pages. As well as Edgell Rickword, Amabel Williams-Ellis, Alick West, Ralph Fox and Douglas Garman, who were involved in the production of the magazine, W. H. Auden, Eric Gill, Storm Jameson, Naomi Mitchison, John Lehmann, Charles Madge, Arthur Calder Marshall, Sylvia Townsend Warner, Stephen Spender, Winifred Holtby, John Strachey, Anthony Blunt, Lewis Grassic Gibbon, Allen Lane, Jack Lindsay, Edward Upward, Pamela Hansford Johnson, A. L. Lloyd, Nancy Cunard, Phyllis Bentley, Osbert Sitwell, A. L. Morton, James Hanley, Rex Warner, George Barker, Ralph Bates and Hugh MacDiarmid are among the many who produced material at various times for *Left Review*.

Left Review was founded by Writers' International, a movement of revolutionary writers and others who 'desire to ally themselves more closely with the class that will build social-ism', as the statement founding the British section put it in February 1934, and the magazine united these diverse talents around the need to stop fascism and radically to change the world. This was understood in an immediate, practical way. First and most obviously, like any professional association or trade union, writers were asked to act politically in their col-lective interest as writers. Thus in the December 1934 issue, for example, a fund was launched to fight for the freedom of imprisoned writers, named after the German writer Erich Mühsam, who had been killed in Oranienburg concentration camp. C. Day Lewis put the relation between the People's Front and writers very directly:

> if English writers are not willing to forgo some of their cherished 'independence,' they will inevitably lose every stitch of the liberty that at present they stand up in. Democracy is everywhere threat-ened. If the house of democracy falls, the fire of art – so nobly fed by the great line of English writers – will be extinguished with it.
> (II, 13: 672)

Writers had to play their part as citizens, and the Spanish Civil War made many of them realise this; 'it has served', as the editorial of January 1937 said, 'to bring to many "intellectuals" a closer sense of their duties as social beings' (II, 16: 857).

More fundamental than their immediately political role, writers in their activity *as writers* were considered to be politi-cal. Literature was not merely a reflection but a part of life, an agent of revolutionary change and an activator of the great reserves of human potential. C. Day Lewis argued with idealis-tic fervour that involvement in the People's Front would improve writers' work:

> as literature draws its nourishment from the life of the people and as its ideology is deeply affected by the social conditions of its age, so it is in the interest of the writer to establish connection with this life and to fight for conditions more favourable to his art. As a member of the People's Front, he will not only be playing the most effective possible part in the struggle to defend culture; he will also be brought into contact with a diversity of men and women, a variety of opinion, aspiration and experience which cannot fail to enrich his own work. This does not mean that he will be either a parasite on the popular organisation or a mere attached correspondent of it. He

will give his special powers and outlook to the movement; and he will receive from it the sense of community which alone can enable him to re-establish the social function of his art. (II, 13: 674)

Ernest Hemingway is an example. Edgell Rickword wrote of Hemingway's recovery from decadence after going to Spain and helping to make the film *Spanish Earth*:

> If we wrote him off as lost after the hunting book, that shows that we had underestimated the power that experience of nobility and heroism has to restore the humanity in a man. It is the Spanish people and the fighters of the International Brigade who have given back Hemingway to himself, to literature and to civilisation.

And at the second Congress of American writers (June 1937), 'he did something which was probably less congenial to him than the fearless things he did in Spain, he made his first public speech' (III, 14: 881).

Politics was part of a whole-culture approach. Thus among the adverts in *Left Review* was one for a socialist primary school which offered progressive education combined with 'a definite social philosophy' based on achieving a classless society, the idea of production for use not profit, equal opportunities and the principle that 'Society should be based on common ownership and the shared social responsibility which it involves' (III, 3: 192). Politics and the arts interact and historically the arts have played a potent political role. If the People's Front 'is developed with a nation-wide enthusiasm', said the editorial of November 1936, 'it will affect not merely governmental policy but our whole culture – just as a hundred years ago the continuous struggle to achieve democratic rights was reflected and encouraged by vigorous movements in religion, literature, and science' (II, 14: 730).

Literary work, in influencing people's attitudes and judgements, was practical in a way beyond the considerations of traditional literary studies. That meant that the subject of discussion had a real-life importance for critics, and their disagreements about literature were seen as consequential. A poor realisation of character could restrict a novel's power to move people toward revolution; an exaggeration of plot could trivialise the dangers of fascism. *Left Review* was willing to make judgements that combined literature and politics, without losing any sophistication or diminishing the importance of the specific skills involved in cultural production (Rickword and Garman, after all, had made their reputation as critics when they edited *The Calendar of Modern Letters* in the mid-1920s).[1]

The continuum of literature and politics was perhaps most clearly expressed in *Left Review*'s final editorial. The occasion naturally called for a review of the contribution the magazine had made to political progress. Appropriately, notice was taken of the seven *Left Review* writers who had joined the International Brigade to defend the Spanish Republic (four of them killed in action), and the perception of the unity of their art and politics is clear:

> Fox wrote shortly before his death: 'Our fate as a people is being decided to-day. It is our fortune to have been born at one of those moments in history which demand from each one of us as an individual that he makes his private decision.' These men had made their decision, and it was the same decision which led them to found and work on *Left Review* and took them ultimately to fight in Spain. (III, 16: 959)

A single motive had made them active in art and politics; art and politics were only different aspects of the same humane and revolutionary struggle.

Discovering Marxist Criticism

Political tension, the need to make a practical contribution to current struggles, was a source of energy for *Left Review*, but there was also the excitement that came from new thinking. The sense of adventure may be difficult to realise today, but *Left Review* was charting completely new territory, without paths or precedents. At the time there was not yet any Marxist literary criticism in English – they were creating it. There was no tradition of Marxist cultural thinking and little of what Marx and Engels had written had been translated into English (Marxist texts were starting to appear in greater number – the 'Publications Received' of *Labour Monthly* for March 1935 listed works by Plekhanov, Lenin and, individually and jointly, Marx and Engels – but still not much was available). As Eric Cook wrote of T. A. Jackson's Marxist critique of Dickens (*Charles Dickens: The Progress of a Radical*, 1937), 'Marxist literary criticism is a field where all are pioneers' (III, 5: 304).

It might be said that there was a predecessor in the magazine *Viewpoint*, which had only two issues, both in 1934: the
earlier issues of *Left Review* had a statement that it incorpor-
ated *Viewpoint*. Describing itself as 'a revolutionary review of
the arts', *Viewpoint* in the second number was explicit in its
direction against fascist culture, which it attacked as represented in Wyndham Lewis and also F. R. Leavis. But the
character of the publication's aesthetic thinking and its radical-
ism were very different from the disciplined, movement politics
and social-functional perspective on the arts that launched *Left
Review*. '*Viewpoint* stands for militant communism and for
individualism and metaphysics in the arts', the first editorial
announced;

> It declares that the work of art is an organic individual creation and
> that it can only exist in its integrity in a classless society, in a
> completely communistic state; that art must become the production
> and property of all. (I, 1: 1)

Politically, *Viewpoint* reflected the old 'class-against-class' attitude: 'the labour parties, on account of their reformist policy of
class collaboration, are steadily paving the way for fascism' (I,
2: 29).

The literary understanding being developed by *Left Review*'s
contributors was impelled by the crisis of the time; the magazine saw the need for broad unity, a popular front. The literary
and artistic theory they made was not abstract; it came out of
their own experience of literature and of politics. Marxism,
because it could make a unified, understandable pattern out of
the separate pieces of experience, was immediately relevant to
criticism as well as politics. It was exciting and it was *new*.

Left Review was no mere propaganda vehicle, such as the
caricature of 1930s Marxist criticism imposed by the Cold War
would suggest. Contrary to the prejudice that politics obscures
or simplifies literary qualities, *Left Review*'s politics gave it
strength because it was coupled with the demand for literary
integrity. Thomas Hodgkin (1911–82) begins a review of four
novels in the December 1937 issue by citing Ralph Fox's principle that the novelist should be a historian, concerned with
the process of change and that 'it is man, active within the
process, that should be the subject-matter of the novel, rather
than the process in its external aspect' (III, 11: 690). He then
invokes Fox again in his critique of *Breakfast in Bed* by Alec

Brown, a *Left Review* contributor who tended to see everything through the filter of class conflict:

> This story seems a good example of what Ralph Fox argued that a novel ought not to be. You are shown the external circumstances of change, but there is no movement in the lives of individual characters: most of them are crude types – Party members with thin lips, firm jaws, and whimsical smiles; wicked bourgeois who openly curse the League of Nations and carry on class-war across the dinner table. The author has not much sense of the lights and shades of character, and not much understanding of society outside the walls of small country houses and service flats. (III, 11: 692)

Edgell Rickword has a more specifically political critical response to André Malraux's novel *Days of Contempt*, not because of its political position, but because it lacks the particularity of human truth which might give it greater literary credibility as well as great political efficacy:

> In Malraux's book the Nazis only appear as an exterior fate, they have no comprehensible motivation for their brutality. We shall not be in a position to combat fascist influence unless we realise the power of the vaguely idealistic jumble of ideas which forms the basis of its mass appeal, as distinct from its very formidable recruitment of sadists. (II, 12: 660)

C. Day Lewis, an important contributor, comes in for criticism himself from Thomas Hodgkin for not being able to convert his political understanding into novelistic experience:

> No one could accuse Day Lewis of isolation. But his book makes grimly plain how much more difficult it is for the average English public-school and university-educated novelist to apply his understanding of social processes to novel-writing than it is to understand those processes. (III, 10: 628)

Slogans were no substitute for a fully realised experience, and it was often made clear that a revolutionary attitude did not justify literary incompetence. In a manner similar to Rickword's, Randall Swingler (the editor from July 1937) criticised a novel about the German underground by someone who had escaped from a concentration camp (*Fires Underground* by Heinz Liepmann): 'The Revolutionary movement

in Germany, as elsewhere, owes much to its writers, but it
has also suffered a lot from pretentious scribblers and journalists on the make' (II, 11: 597). Political posture was not
enough. In a similar vein, Sylvia Townsend Warner takes a
mocking tone toward those who adopt the label without
grasping the substance. Reviewing a concert of Soviet music,
she wrote, 'An audience anxious to applaud anything from
U.S.S.R. gave itself away by applauding too vigorously what
was most reminiscent of the dear old music of capitalist
Russia' (I, 9: 384). The problem of attention to the label
rather than the thing itself is also raised in Edgell Rickword's critique of David Daiches's *Literature and Society*,
which was a Left Book Club selection. Daiches's 'failure', he
says, is due not just to 'incidental lapses (which in a survey
of seven hundred years would be excusable), but to an insuf-
ficiently concrete appreciation of the works themselves and
the conditions under which they were produced' (III, 14:
890). The same demand for concreteness is made in regard
to critical writing. Douglas Garman rejects the imposition of
Marxist generalisations without sufficient attention to specif-
ics; in reviewing *5 on Revolutionary Art*, he says Klingender's
essay suffers from 'the most common defect of communist
writing, jargon', and he accuses Klingender of being in 'too
great hurry to show immediate, concrete results from a study
that must necessarily be tentative and laborious'. And he is
critical of 'the mechanical way in which Klingender applies
his method'. This is not the fault of the Marxist approach,
he says: Klingender's insistence on 'the fundamental concepts
of materialism ... is in stimulating contrast to much vague
thinking for which Marx is too often held responsible' (II, 4:
183).

Political Line

There can be no doubt about the political motive of *Left
Review*'s criticism, but even the most servile writer would
have found it hard to follow the line on literature. There
were strong political judgements but there was no uniformity; contributors to the magazine were constantly arguing
about what should be done. There was no line. The distin-
guishing quality of a line is that it imposes particular conclusions, whatever actual examination turns up, and forces

material into one interpretative frame. A political project as broad as *Left Review*'s – stopping fascism – does not lend itself to the directional focus that would constitute a line.

Political conformity was not part of the character of *Left Review* (apart from admiration for the Soviet Union – which in any case was not given without criticism), nor did the magazine show any rigidity in critical approach. The nearest it came to presenting a literary-theoretical line was the address to Soviet writers by Dimitrov, leader of the Communist International, which *Left Review* printed in June 1935 (it is reprinted here in Section II). Dimitrov was celebrated as a hero for his defence in the Reichstag trial, but, quite reasonably, was not seen as an expert on literature. He did say that literature must be placed 'at the service of the proletarian revolution' and 'must serve the great revolutionary ideal of millions of workers', but he did not say in what manner. Insofar as it gave an ultimate purpose, it may perhaps be considered to be a 'line', but it offered no prescriptions and not much direction. *Left Review*'s attitude is perhaps indicated by the reviewing space allocated to Dimitrov's biography (*Dimitrov* by Stella D. Blagoyeva), reviewed with four other books by Tom Wintringham, one of *Left Review*'s editors: 'I have left too little space for Dimitrov and Chapayev. The book on the former is worthy of its subject; more need scarcely be said' (I, 7: 283). Two of the other books reviewed were the Marx–Engels correspondence and Engels's *Anti-Dühring*, which in the context would seem to deserve considerable space; if Dimitrov had been regarded as giving the lead in literature as in politics, then surely he would have been accorded more space. Dimitrov's great achievement was bringing the Comintern to a popular front policy; he is undoubtedly a political, but not a cultural, leader. As an intelligent, though not expert, reader of literature (like Marx and Engels), he thought his own experience in the Reichstag trial a fine subject for fiction (heroic but not individualistic, which would make it a good model, and a focus of social movements, which would make it a good opportunity for analysis or propaganda). Ralph Fox apparently was also taken with the idea, and in *The Novel and the People* (1937) described at length the novel that could be made from Dimitrov's experience.

Marx and Engels provided the ideological approach, but not a method. The fundamental principle of the literary criticism that derives from the writings of Marx and Engels is the often-quoted statement from Marx's preface to *A Contribution to 'the Critique of Political Economy'* (1859):

In the social production of their means of existence men enter into
definite, necessary relations which are independent of their will,
productive relationships which correspond to a definite stage of development of their material productive forces. The aggregate of these
productive relationships constitutes the economic structure of society, the real basis on which a juridical and political superstructure
arises, and to which definite forms of social consciousness correspond. The mode of production of the material means of existence
conditions the whole process of social, political and intellectual life.
It is not the consciousness of men that determines their existence,
but, on the contrary, it is their social existence that determines their
consciousness.[2]

This classic statement served fruitfully as the basis for much
Marxist literary criticism, but it was also possible to reduce it
to a simplistic correlation of social structure and artistic production, class and consciousness. In reviewing *The Intelligentsia
of Great Britain* by Dmitri Mirsky, a book that sets out to
expose fascist bias among British intellectuals, Alick West details how Mirsky's approach is simplistic. Mirsky is wrong to
dismiss H. G. Wells as fascist, says West: 'To emphasize the
Fascist side, is perfectly right; but to say nothing about the
other is to misrepresent Wells' actual function and miss an
opportunity.' Similarly for Mirsky's treatment of Huxley and
Lawrence, which 'is always the explanation only in terms of
capitalist decay. But there is no simple, direct transposition of
capitalist decay into literature' (I, 8: 327).
    In general the writers of *Left Review* rejected the idea that
individual behaviour could be read off from class position, but
class was fundamental for discussion of whole historical
periods. As A. L. Morton said in a review of two historical
books, 'Individuals often act disinterestedly but classes do not,
and, in the last resort, it is classes and not individuals who
make history.' He extended this idea later in the same review:

Historical materialism, in short, does not deny that moral convictions exist or that they play an important historical role. It does deny
that classes become seized with moral (or any other) ideas arbitrarily
and independently. (III, 13: 814, 816)

Left Review understood very well that art is complex and has a
complex relation to the world in which it is generated. Rickword's review of Upton Sinclair's *Mammonart* suggests as early

as the second number of *Left Review* that the role of class in literary reception is important but cannot be regarded as an adequate explanation of literature:

> What bourgeois education teaches us to call the best art is, I am prepared to agree, what has proved the most successful propaganda at some date in history; and the most successful propaganda is, naturally, that which exemplifies or deodorizes the ideology of the ruling class. That is the main contention of *Mammonart* and it can be supported by many examples, but it does not exhaust the functions and achievements of art.

Rickword finally calls *Mammonart* a 'romantic aberration containing some sound notions badly mishandled' (I, 2: 45).

Certainly there was some mechanistic thinking in *Left Review* and some reductive treatment of the relationship between being and consciousness. Charles Madge, for example, wrote in the April 1937 issue:

> If the novelist has any function in our age, it is to delineate the relationship of an individual to his class, on the basis of scientific materialism. While this function remains in abeyance, the novel will be no more than a plaything or a drug. It demands the most clear-cut and direct approach which can be found. (III, 3: 183)

Jack Lindsay, a phenomenally productive writer and frequent contributor to *Left Review*, tends also to reductive thinking. Thus he says of Brecht's *Threepenny Opera*, 'The enormously complicated and uproarious story of intrigue and villainy in Brecht's ironic masterpiece is but the simple statement of what is going on all the while behind the capitalist façade' (III, 3: 179). Caricature as a powerful critical device disappears in Lindsay's reading – the work is reduced to information, to exposé. It is not so much that Lindsay neglects particularity but that he neglects the literary experience – the emotional *process* that takes place in reading the book – for a general political conclusion. In the same piece Lindsay praises an American novel, *The Tomato Field* by Stuart Engstrand, for its development of 'the theme of the class-struggle':

> There is a further point about this book worth making. It deals with an episode in the class-war in exactly the right way. It does not base itself on merely picturing miseries and frustrations, nor does it go to the

other extreme of assuming a revolutionary spirit in its readers. It takes a concrete instance, and shows how the workers can tackle and master it. As a worker wrote to me recently: 'It is no use describing life on the dole to an unemployed man; he appreciates all this sympathy, but he wants to see the way out, to have the fundamentals of the class-struggle constantly underlined.' Yet at the same time the writer must realise, while addressing himself *to* the workers, that 'the mass of them are not fully class conscious.' I think this is excellent advice. (III, 3: 179)

The writers of *Left Review*, with few exceptions, were involved in arousing class consciousness – but most of them recognised that the problem was interpreting the material of daily life in a wider frame rather than imposing at one go sweeping political conclusions. If the terms are recognised as complex, then 'being-determines-consciousness' provides a rich source for theoretical development. The excitement of the 'discovery' of Gramsci in the 1960s, the recognition of the power and intricacy of cultural forces, is partly also the feeling of expansiveness at the liberation from simplistic Marxism. It is that sense of potential that animates *Left Review*, and the magazine was dealing as early as the 1930s with questions that the 'post-political' Marxists of the 1970s and 1980s, in their 'liberation of the text', thought themselves to be raising for the first time. In *Left Review* the de-stabilising of the idea of art as pure reflection, as a mirror of reality, can be seen in articles that do not usually have a theoretical focus. Thus Randall Swingler, in a move to reclaim revolutionary culture, begins with an article on William Blake; he brings questions of reality that had troubled poets since Baudelaire into the context of revolution, making an argument that is theoretical but that never announces itself as theory:

> Even while it has been admitted that the values of poetry come into immediate conflict with the values of capitalist society, it is still supposed that poetry creates a world of its own, a magic world, over against the world of actuality and at no point contiguous upon it. It is precisely because poets, affirming their world to be the real world and the structure of capitalism to be ephemeral and false, fought against the conditioning of their education, that they are important to us. (III, 1: 22)

The accusation (or perhaps, from the establishment viewpoint, praise) that Blake lived in intellectual isolation from the real world is false, says Swingler: 'Blake's unique and rambling forms of expression only become intelligible at all when we realise that they are concrete generalisations in dramatic form of the historical process as it activates within the human individual' (III, 1: 27).

The understanding of the complexity of 'being-determines-consciousness' is seen in practical terms in the explanation that Amabel Williams-Ellis gives to would-be entrants of *Left Review*'s literary competition in the April 1935 issue. In telling readers how they might go about composing their narrative of 'an encounter', she suggests, in only a single page of text, the myriad determinants that could have produced the present:

> What became of all those funny dreams ... How did life really turn out for this one? There was, the writer may be sure, work – or perhaps its horrid counterpart a vain search for work; some sort of love affair; lots of worry, some fun we hope. All these things formed the person that the writer is looking at. Did this man or woman think about everything as it came along, ponder and turn it over: or just live and let things happen? (I, 7: 277)

This is no more than a lead-in to the competition – there is no pretence that it is profound – but it makes clear the awareness that life has to be seen as determined by an enormous number of factors.

Williams-Ellis's perspective in her own criticism also involves looking at the complexity of relationships and takes no condition for granted. Thus, in a review of Olaf Stapledon's *Waking World*, she says the phenomenon of 'Russia's love of tractors and of concrete mixers' does not deserve the mockery it receives from Western readers. What is particularly interesting is not so much her defence of admiration for mechanical power in a peasant setting but the detail in which she suggests how material life in a fully industrialised country can condition readers' responses:

> They drink their tea from mass produced cups so that it is no tragedy if one is broken. They walk on machine made shoes. If the sole of one is cracked in drying after a wet walk, it is again no tragedy. Their minds on higher things, they can be as careless as they like about studs and cuff-links. They have all the pencils and fountain pens, carbons and typing paper that they need for their job, a bus takes them over a smooth road out to the country to see their

friends of a Sunday, or they go to see Mickey Mouse and René Clair. They are so used to these things that they forget the point of view of those who have not got them just as the congregation in a dripping Sunday in England fails to share the psalmist's enthusiasm for cooling streams and fountains. (I, 5: 189)

The sense of complexity of 'being-determines-consciousness' in *Left Review* included the notion of experimentation; literature's function was certainly not to project pre-formed responses for an audience but to introduce ways of looking, models of being, that could be responded to and could also be subjected to questioning. What happened to readers was seen, in effect, as the result of a process, a negotiation of experiences and generalisations. This is the opposite of taking a 'line', which assumes a single right answer, does accept pluralism and prescribes a 'correct' position. The notion of Marxism as scientific was used, paradoxically, to close off plurality and the multiplicity of meaning and value – paradoxically because science depends on testing ideas, on experimentation, on openness to the new (which must be more than the logical conclusion of preexisting facts). But the popular conception of science as answers, as the method of eliminating error, was enlisted to make having an intellectual line seem appropriate. In *Left Review* this can be seen in Charles Madge's subordination of art to science and his view that art only provides material for science (e.g. a novel could be interesting material for a psychologist). Art has a 'concealed' content which science can discover: 'Poetry deals, not with the inexplicable, but with what has not yet been explained. It lights up, by fitful flashes, a scene on which the full day of science will presently dawn' (III, 1: 32). Madge reduces art to a symptom: Picasso and modern artists discovered the primitive nature of mankind and their sense of guilt, which had produced 'ritual excess' in the 'savage', 'now drove the artist to conceal the content of his thought in tortuous and incomprehensible forms'.

The sense of art as a model or transmitter of information, more than a transformer of reality, had considerable theoretical force behind it on the left. In the first issue of the *Modern Quarterly*, in January 1938, a journal with a clear scientific orientation (the 'Editorial Council' was composed of fifteen people, at least eight of whom were distinguished scientists and five were Fellows of the Royal Society), the editorial statement of purpose made art the shadow of science: the aim of the journal was to contribute to a 'system of thought which will correspond to the real world which science analyses and in which we live. In this connection we recognize the arts and sciences as an integral part of the social progress of mankind' (I, 1: 3). The role of art is not very clear, and it is at best secondary.

Left Review had not placed art in opposition to science and generally recognised distinct functions for literature. It was thus more accepting, sometimes enthusiastically so, of literature's emotional logic. In the same discussion of Russians' tractor-love quoted above, Amabel Williams-Ellis tries to understand the Russians as full humans, including their defects, not just as rational products of a rational ideology. Without denying scientific objectivity, she insists that the Russians, and we, are all emotional beings, and that this has positive social functions:

> The present writer suggests that over-estimation is an absolutely necessary mechanism by which alone an organism or a society is able to put its last ounce of enthusiasm and energy into a creative or necessary effort. Couldn't the intellectuals all agree to call certain kinds of enthusiasm by this comparatively long name, and then feel better about such things as the Russians and their tractors? We all do it if we are working hard and willingly, or in love. (I, 5: 190)

Even socialist realism, which may be considered the most 'scientifically'-orientated approach to the arts (Stalin called writers 'the engineers of the human soul'), was treated flexibly in *Left Review*. It was as yet untainted by the doctrinal rigidity it developed later. André Van Gyseghem's 'Letter from Moscow' (reprinted in Section II) talks about what would seem classic socialist realism – 'an intensely realistic play about the building of the Baltic-White-Sea Canal by a crowd of ex-thieves, wreckers and prostitutes under the leadership of the Communist Party' – but presented with 'formal conventional treatment', like Kabuki (the description suggests something that might now be identified as 'Brechtian'). He concludes that the plays he has described are 'a striking instance of the close contact between the theatre and the march of events which exists in the Soviet Union and which results in a living Realistic Theatre,' and he adds, 'Only when we in England are able to show on our stage such projections of contemporary life will our theatre attain true significance' (I, 7: 272, 273). This theatre shares with a conventional socialist realism a positive

INTRODUCTION

attitude toward human potential and to changing the world, but otherwise bears no resemblance to what is usually designated by the term.

Left Review's atmosphere of cultural openness was not without obstacles. The problem of political line appeared clearly in March 1937 with T. A. Jackson's discussion of the Moscow treason trials. Jackson was a prominent Communist Party figure and author of the important Marxist tome, *Dialectics: The Logic of Marxism and Its Critics*, brought out by party publishers, Lawrence and Wishart, in 1936. His review of *Report of Court Proceedings in the Case of the Anti-Soviet Trotskyite Centre* presents the official explanation of how the accused entered on their supposed career of 'anti-Soviet' treason. They lacked faith in the capacity of the Soviet system – which produced first their fear of fascism, then made them try to do a deal with fascism, and finally led them to helping fascism. The argument has a logic which, despite running counter to observed fact, gives it a paranoiac credibility. Karl Radek (who at the 1934 Soviet Writers' Congress had given an extensive, detailed and dialectical explanation of how fascism destroys literature) and two others confessed, wrote Jackson, 'because they saw it was the only rational thing left for them to do' (III, 2: 117). He wrote that every trained lawyer at the trial was 'unhesitatingly and unreservedly convinced of the scrupulous fairness of the trial, and the unquestionable and entire guiltiness of the accused' (III, 2: 116). This is not too great an exaggeration: American journalists thought the trials were open and justifiable and the American ambassador telegraphed the White House that the defendants were guilty. But Jackson's biblical imagery – 'as terrible and as horrible as the fall of Lucifer himself' (III, 2: 118) – suggests more of a witch-hunt. Similarly, J. R. Campbell, later General Secretary of the Communist Party of Great Britain, reviewing a book on Trotsky and the treason trials in December 1937, stigmatises anyone who accepts Trotsky's answer to the charges levelled against him at the Moscow trials: 'The answer will not, however, convince anyone except those anti-Soviet people who want to be convinced' (III, 11: 685). Yet, in the same issue, the demonisation of dissidents as Trotskyites is also presented with a critical irony. Frank Jackson's emphasis in a review of Soviet films suggests that it is overdone: 'This, however, is not the theme of *all* new Russian films' (III, 11: 679).

The line put forward by T. A. Jackson and Campbell is

applied by them only to politics, but Bert Marshall brings it directly into literary judgement. In 'Soviet Poetry', in the November 1937 issue, he dismisses Pasternak, 'considered by some to be the greatest Soviet poet', as being 'far removed from Soviet actuality', writing poems that are 'personal and full of subtle associations which make them difficult, even for cultured Russians to understand', and his poetry is 'still very subjective'. But his rejection of Pasternak comes not from the poetry itself; it comes from the politics of Pasternak's admirers:

> It is significant to note that Bukharin, at the Conference of Writers, implied that the future development of Soviet poetry should be along the line of Pasternak, rather than Mayakovsky, and only after the recent Trials was it made clear that even on the front of culture was there a conscious attempt to stifle the genuine line of Soviet poetry – that is the line of Mayakovsky. (III, 10: 599–600)

Such imposition of judgement is a dangerous short-circuiting of the whole critical process. It is simplistic and is accompanied by an increasingly reductive notion of literature.

Some of the danger can be seen in the attitude that literature needs to be defended – not, as in the earlier editorials, against fascist repression and book-burners but against irrelevance to the revolutionary struggle. The editorial of the March 1938 issue offers a justification of a meeting to celebrate Keats's anniversary held under the auspices of the Hampstead Communist Party, with Stephen Spender as the invited speaker:

> the proper function of a writer is to develop that weapon which Keats wielded for combating the miseries of the world and their causes, and that the greatest writers in our time will be those who write in the highest consciousness of the miseries and potentialities of this world. What more proper then, than for Communists to celebrate one who did in fact develop man's consciousness of his struggle against reaction in whatever form? (III, 14: 832)

Keats has a secure place in the development of the humane culture which the Writers' International seeks to defend; there is no need to force upon him a revolutionary role. A reduction to banner-waving minimises the literary and also the political value of his poetry – and negates the qualities that earlier *Left*

Review had recognised as fundamental to literature's revolutionary potential.

This distrust of the open and testing quality of culture is seen also in the changing character of readers' competitions. *Left Review* had a genuinely popular practice that was a consistent reflection of its theoretical perspective. It encouraged its readers to try writing themselves, to reflect on their experience and make it available to others. The assumption in the practice of the editors was that many people have something interesting to say; the theoretical assumption was that the neat distinction between producers and consumers of culture is largely artificial and damaging to both individuals and society. Most of the early issues included the editorial note, 'every endeavour will be made to return contributions if rejected, and also to make whatever criticism seems likely to help the contributor' (I, 1: 2). While only a few of the reader-writers went on to literary careers, considerable numbers must have been given strength by the experience, realising productive capacities that previously had not had an outlet, and many others gained at least a democratic sense of the legitimacy of making their own critical judgements. (Material from the competition settings and reports is reprinted in Section V.)

The emphasis on 'the possible' in fictional construction, which Amabel Williams-Ellis presented, was replaced by a narrower topic that attracts limited political reasoning (e.g. 'On Taking Politics Seriously') or by an entirely non-fictional demand, such as answering in not more than 200 words four questions on 'What Life Could Mean to Me'. The competitions move from an open, democratic spirit, through 'democracy' strongly controlled from the centre, to none at all.

But the prescriptive attitude did not dominate the magazine and should be kept in perspective. The absence of any official party position on culture and the fact that Marxist criticism was uncharted territory were probably what allowed *Left Review* to remain flexible and creative (i.e. it was constrained where policy was already formulated, free where it was not); but the *positive* impetus to remain flexible is probably connected to the magazine's emphasis on creative writing and graphics. In terms of space in the magazine, slightly less than half would seem to have been original creative work. Criticism was certainly important (and generated the most heat) but its function was seen as dependent on original creativity – the imaginative experience was more important than the critical commentary. There was no premium on elaborated abstraction; on the contrary, the status of criticism was enhanced by its involvement with real living, and literary theory did not usually appear in isolation but was embedded in discussion and attached to examples. In part this can be attributed to the absence of Marxist theoretical texts and the framework for discussion which they could provide, which meant that critics had to work from concrete examples. This gave their discussion a clarity which unfortunately has not usually been valued by subsequent theorists.

For a publication committed to a political position, *Left Review* was surprisingly undogmatic. Certainly there were intemperate quarrels – Ralph Fox attacked Francis Klingender as 'Colonel Blimp Klingender' for his views on art – but they were not based on dogma. In fact the individualism of the literary judgements made in the magazine is often surprising. C. Day Lewis, for example, expressed great admiration for T. S. Eliot's *Waste Land*, and the various views of socialist realism that appeared in *Left Review*'s pages indicate the absence of a particular dogma in that area. Orwell, long regarded with hostility by the Communist Party, is treated even-handedly, even favourably, in a review of *The Road to Wigan Pier* by Derek Kahn, assistant editor of the magazine. He mentions that Orwell criticises 'Socialists in general, and the *Left Review* in particular for cant about the decay of bourgeois culture which conflicts with the bourgeois content of their own lives'. Even so, Kahn finds praise for Orwell: 'The author's generalisations are weak, but his observation is keen and his sincerity fascinating – it is this sincerity which gives documentary value to the work.' He is critical without being confrontational or seeking to impose a 'correct' position: 'No doubt if Mr. Orwell extended his investigations so as to include the established organisations of the working-class he would emerge with a conception of Socialism more in keeping with present realities' (III, 3: 186, 187). *Left Review*'s articles do not offer themselves as the last word; they are contributions to what is recognised as an ongoing process. And the magazine was witty, the quality probably most antagonistic to dogmatism. Thus the magazine's advertising sent itself up, even though it had to serve the same persuasive role as normal advertising. The subscription advert on the back cover of III, 14, for example, began with an echo of Dale Carnegie – 'Win Your Friends and

Influence People' – transformed by the addition – 'to read *Left
Review* and subscribe to it.' The addresses to readers, the
adverts for subscribers and the prominence of cartoons by 'the
3 Jameses' – Boswell, Fitton and Holland – all had a lightness
and ironic sense that gave personality to the publication and
made any attempts at a line seem marginal.

The Achievement of Left Review

Was there any lasting achievement of *Left Review* or was it just
ephemeral brilliance? As part of the People's Front, *Left Review*
played a role in helping to stop fascism (although it had
stopped publishing even before the outbreak of World War II).
It involved large numbers of people in cultural activity and
forged an important link for them between culture and democracy. *Left Review* did not succeed in making a proletarian
culture but, along with the Left Book Club, it did much to
democratise it. As Stephen Spender wrote in his introduction
to *Poems for Spain*, which he edited with John Lehmann, 'The
conditions for a great popular poetry are not yet obtained;
what we note is the desire for such a poetry' (p. 9). It did not
condescend to its readers, it did not promote any sentimental
abandonment of standards, but it was accessible to ordinary
people. *Left Review* and the Left Book Club made a significant
contribution to the landmark Labour victory in 1945.

    Left Review was democratic in more than just today's sense
that people are free to do what they like; it was also democratic in a collective sense of a group greater than the sum of
the parts, which gives identity to people while assuring their
rights as individuals. This underlies the tribute to Ralph Fox
signed by twenty-nine members of the International Association of Writers for the Defence of Culture in the February
1937 issue:

> He had much personal ambition, but he did not believe in the
> sanctity of his individual talent, and so was willing to give up his life
> to suppress that which he believed threatens all individuals, all
> talents, all creation – reaction in its latest, most detestable form,
> Fascism. (III, 1: 4)

In its cultural production, *Left Review* made an enduring
contribution to the development of Marxist literary criticism,

theorising the role and function of literature, presenting a more or less coherent explanation of literature as a social phenomenon, and raising questions about the nature of literature's social value that are still alive in discussion today. It also offered penetrating critiques of authors that are still canonical – such as Spender, West and Rickword on Joyce, Eliot and Lawrence.

From the impetus of *Left Review* grew the foundation works of English Marxist literary criticism – *Crisis in Criticism*, *The Novel and the People*, and *Illusion and Reality*. West and Fox were very active in *Left Review*, as writers and editors, and Caudwell (1907–37), although not involved with the magazine except for a posthumously published open letter to W. H. Auden, was very much influenced by it. His thinking in *Illusion and Reality*, the single most important work of British Marxist criticism, and also in much of his *Studies in a Dying Culture* and *Further Studies in a Dying Culture*, derives from material published in *Left Review*. C. Day Lewis's 'Revolutionaries and Poetry' (the first selection reprinted in Section II), in particular, finds an echo in *Illusion and Reality*, as does Amabel Williams-Ellis's emphasis on the social character of literature's emotion and the importance of reception by an audience (e.g. her introduction to the first competition in I, 1).

One of the strengths of the Marxism of the Communist Party Historians' Group, said Eric Hobsbawm, 'was never to reduce history to a simple economic or "class interest" determinism, or to devalue politics and ideology'.[3] This applies equally to the Marxism of *Left Review*. The non-dogmatic Marxism of the Historians' Group, says Hobsbawm, can be attributed in fair measure to their interest in literature. In the case of *Left Review*, literature was seen as both past record and future possibility, as encouragement to action and as careful weighing of consequences. It was make-believe but real, insubstantial but emotionally powerful, out of time but immediate, intensely individual yet highly social. Seen through the filter of revolution, literature was in no way diminished. Revolution, building socialism, was for most *Left Review* contributors a magnificent vision, focusing the distinctly human qualities of purpose and desire.

Why did this success come to a sudden end? In the next to last number there was a notice: 'The considerable success of *Left Review* has made it clear that the opportunity now exists

for the launching of a monthly in a highly popular form
addressed to a wide public – to all mentally alive people in
fact' (III, 15: 900). The details were promised for the next
month, and the final editorial explained the situation:

> The first issue of *Left Review* appeared in October 1934. With this, the
> May issue of 1938 and the final issue of Volume Three, *Left Review*, as
> you have known it, ceases publication. Not because it has proved a
> failure, or because its first success is declining. Precisely for the
> opposite reason. Paradoxically it comes to an end at the height of its
> success, and because of that success. Its history has been a gradually
> mounting graph of influence and position. Now it is felt by the
> Editorial Board that the present basis of editorial work, production and
> distribution, is too narrow to cope adequately with the job and the
> opportunities that press so urgently upon us.

So many people had become politically active in the field of
culture, the editorial goes on to say, that 'to provide an organ
for the life-utterance of a people's will in the people's interest,
is now beyond the task of a review privately run on voluntary
labour'. *Left Review* will close 'so that we may give all our
energy in support of a wider project, which can reach a vastly
greater mass of the people' which will follow the same principle that has governed the magazine, namely: 'that the vitality
of a whole culture depends upon the unity of interest of a
whole people, and the opportunity for free expression of their
unity and their will' (III, 16: 957, 959–60).
    This is stirring stuff but it is still not entirely clear why
Left Review had to close. Andy Croft has traced the history
and says that, because of its identification with the Communist Party, *Left Review* was unlikely to increase its circulation
beyond 5,000 a month: 'To make the magazine more popular, more secure and more professionally produced, Swingler
(clearly with the sanction of King Street) closed *Left Review*
in order to put it at the disposal of the wider movement it
had helped to bring into existence.'[4] Negotiations were carried to a late stage with Penguin, but nothing came of it
finally. The magazine was announced for September 1938 but
it never appeared.
    There was probably a good deal of ill-luck in the failure
to achieve the new magazine, but there may also have been
a lack of enthusiasm among Communist Party leadership.
This, rather than failed ambition, may be what was

ultimately responsible for *Left Review*'s closure. The description of the purpose of art and science, its subjects, in the advert for the new magazine, is worth noting: 'The purpose of Art and Science is to sharpen and direct our experience, to mobilise our powers *for action*' (III, 16: 967). The emphasis suggests a reductive view of literature quite different from the flexible understanding that characterised *Left Review*; it is perhaps more in character with some of the late attempts to impose a line in the magazine.

At a point when the contradictions between Popular Front attitudes and the convolutions of official, Soviet-led positions were growing, the open, independent, questioning Marxism of *Left Review* was probably not congenial to the leadership of the party. And despite heroic efforts by some of the Party's literary intellectuals, the period of Britain's most creative Marxism was brought to an end.

Notes

1. *The Calendar of Modern Letters* ran from March 1925 to July 1927, publishing, among the work of other notable writers and critics, stories by D. H. Lawrence. F. R. Leavis selected and introduced a collection of essays from *The Calendar*, entitled *Towards Standards of Criticism* (London: Wishart & Co., 1933), and paid tribute to its excellence by naming his own *Scrutiny* after the 'Scrutinies', re-examinations of literary figures, that appeared in *The Calendar*.
2. *A Handbook of Marxism*, ed. Emile Burns (London: Victor Gollancz, 1935), pp. 371–2.
3. *Rebels and Their Causes*, ed. Maurice Cornforth (London: Lawrence & Wishart, 1978), p. 38.
4. 'Get a Grip Lads!: The Story of Fore Publications', p. 5, in Andy Croft, ed., forthcoming book on the Communist Party and culture (London: Pluto Press). No. 16 King Street was the headquarters of the Communist Party.

I.   The Writers' International Controversy

Left Review was begun as a *cultural* response to a political situation, the rise of fascism and the danger to democracy perceived in Britain. It was set up by the Writers' International, British Section, which was itself established at a conference in February 1934.

The position statement of the Writers' International foundation conference was published in the first issue of *Left Review*. It pointed to the 'triviality' and 'decadence' of British culture and related the cultural problem to the world political and economic crisis. The cultural crisis was the counterpart of the collapse of capitalism. All the best in culture was threatened by fascism; it could be protected and developed only by socialism. Writers were called on to form a revolutionary socialist organisation:

> There is a crisis of ideas in the capitalist world to-day not less considerable than the crisis in economics.
>
> Increasing numbers of people are reading seriously, trying to get some insight as to the causes of events that are shattering the world they know, and some understanding of the reasons for men's actions. And increasingly they are being given, not insight or understanding, but 'distraction.' Journalism, literature, the theatre, are developing in technique while narrowing in content; they cannot escape their present triviality until they deal with the events and issues that matter; the death of an old world and the birth of a new.
>
> The decadence of the past twenty years of English literature and the theatre cannot be understood apart from all that separates 1913 and 1934. It is the collapse of a culture, accompanying the collapse of an economic system.
>
> There are already a number of writers who realize this; they desire and are working for the ending of the capitalist order of

society. They aim at a new order based not on property and profit, but on co-operative effort. They realize that the working class will be the builders of this new order, and see that the change must be revolutionary in effect. Even those to whom politics are secondary desire to ally themselves more closely with the class that will build socialism.

It is time for these, together with the working-class journalists and writers who are trying to express the feelings of their class, to organize an association of revolutionary writers such as the association already formed in the United States (where there is the John Reed Club with Dreiser, Dos Passos and Sherwood Anderson) and in France (the A. E. A. R., with André Gide, Barbusse, Aragon, etc.). Such an association obviously should apply for affiliation to the International of Revolutionary Writers, which has among its more famous members Maxim Gorky, Ludwig Renn, Romain Rolland and Upton Sinclair.

The statement then put forward criteria for membership, which had a clearer element of party-political line – support for the Soviet Union as well as alliance with the working class. The invitation to join was extended to writers in three overlapping categories; those

(a) who see in the development of Fascism the terrorist dictatorship of dying capitalism and a menace to all the best achievements of human culture, and consider that the best in the civilization of the past can only be preserved and further developed by joining in the struggle of the working class for a new socialist society; who are opposed to all attempts to hinder unity in the struggle or any retreat before Fascism or compromise with fascist tendencies;

(b) who, if members of the working class, desire to express in their work, more effectively than in the past, the struggle of their class;

(c) who will use their pens and their influence against imperialist war and in defence of the Soviet Union, the State where the foundations of Socialism have already been laid, and will expose the hidden forms of war being carried on against the Indian, Irish, African and Chinese peoples.

Readers of *Left Review* were asked for their comments on the statement. In the third issue, December 1934, the statement was reprinted with the first batch of discussion contributions, under the heading 'Writers' International Controversy'. The argument was continued through the next three numbers, ending in March 1935. The pieces were all short but raised fundamental questions about the nature of literature, the relation between literature and society, and the political responsibility of writers. 'Controversy' was an appropriate title – there was little agreement and considerable dispute – but it served to open major issues. It brought to the surface and articulated attitudes that affected the practical activity of writers.

There were fifteen contributions, including pieces by two of the three editors of *Left Review* at the time (Montagu Slater and T. H. Wintringham),   C. Day Lewis, Lewis Grassic Gibbon and Hugh MacDiarmid. 'Writers and Manifestos' by Stephen Spender in number 5, while not included as part of the controversy, commented on the same issues.

The most controversial piece was Alec Brown's hard-line, mechanistic view of literature, which appeared in the first group of contributors (issue number 3) and was frequently cited later. His suggested slogan 'literary English from Caxton to us is an artificial jargon of the ruling class' served as a model of a reductive class-war position where political line always takes precedence over free, open consideration of literature's functioning in a specific situation. The crude argument and categorical dismissal of so much of literature may have served, better than a more subtle attempt, to highlight the inadequacy of conclusions which are drawn before the evidence is examined and generalisations which are made without reference to detailed, specific understanding.

In the following number Montagu Slater placed in context the issues that Brown had dealt with in a mechanical way. He offered long quotations from Marx, but as a means of opening problems rather than stopping discussion by citing authority. In number 5 Hugh MacDiarmid also took Alec Brown to task, but from a more specialised perspective, criticising Brown's limited views on language.

C. Day Lewis (in number 4) viewed political behaviour in a longer perspective; he affirmed political commitment but stressed that the method of literature (as opposed to journalism) is indirect, and he objected to the crude imposition of political positions on the arts. He also said that the important thing was for writers to go beyond espousing revolutionary positions and to put them into practice. This theme was continued in number 5 by Lewis Grassic Gibbon, who made a more direct attack on those who impose on literature criteria that are predominantly political, whose ignorance is shielded by revolutionary slogans. Membership of a union of revolutionary writers, he said, must be based on literary professionalism, not just revolutionary fervour. He adds an aggressive note to what was otherwise quite restrained debate, using phrases like 'bolshevik blah' and 'moronic envy'.

While Grassic Gibbon emphasised the creation of literature, in the same number Douglas Garman went in the opposite direction, giving priority to criticism. Criticism in his view had the politically important job of clarifying social issues – criticising 'the pretentious humbug of democratic culture' in popular fiction and film and identifying the less obvious ways, such as cultural perspective, in which the movement toward fascism was taking place. Marxism had to be applied, not as political dogma, but as analysis of the social phenomena embodied in the experience presented by literature. He saw this as the one task that *Left Review* was in a unique position to carry out.

The contributions of Brown, Montagu Slater, C. Day Lewis, Grassic Gibbon, Douglas Garman and Hugh MacDiarmid are printed in the order in which they originally appeared.

From Alec Brown [December 1934]

All normal writing has a reading public in view. The starting point of any comments on this programme must be clarity as to *for whom are we writing?* The answer must surely be that all our writing has one end in view, the revolutionary end of establishing a socialist republic, that is a working-class democracy. The second group (b) of prospective members ought of course to come first. The membership clause need be no more than: 'members of the working class or those of other classes who have crossed over and allied themselves to the working-class, who use the written (or printed) word for furthering their share in the labour of establishing a workers' republic.'

But that still is not what we are going to DO, and I get back to the question: WHOM ARE WE WRITING FOR AND HOW? The answer is that we have primarily in view the working-class reading public.

This reading public cannot afford to buy many books; and there are not many books fit for them to buy. It is up to us to tackle both of these problems. As I see it the vast jellyfish of the petty middle-class is a lesser problem, though that must be the class the committee has in mind when it talks about a 'crisis of ideas.' So my suggestions boil down to three.

Suggestion 1. A special investigation permanently to be carried on to deal with the provision of the broad masses of the working-class with what constructive revolutionary literature is and will be available. I should suggest detailing a special member or members to enquire into the possibility of much more use of parallel cheap paper editions of books. It must be shown that this parallel paper edition will not lessen sales of the expensive edition and will pay. And we should do something really practical about organizing contacts between us all, and especially between those of us with a pure working-class position, and those starting with both the advantage and the serious handicap of bourgeois beginnings.

Suggestion 2. We need a permanent propaganda committee, to work towards

a. the proletarianisation of our outlook (of those of us who have bourgeois origins in our work) – and during the initial period of our magazine, most important, to carry on rigorous contemptuous criticism of all highbrowism, intellectualism, abstract rationalism and similar dilettanteisms; in short, a constant goading question to be there, the single-minded question (the marxist question) ARE WE AN ORGANIZATION OF REVOLUTIONARY WRITERS OR ARE WE NOT?

b. OF NO SMALL IMPORTANCE, the proletarianisation of our actual language, by which I mean getting right down to spoken English in our work. No small task, because plain English folk can't understand the jargon most of us put out, and there I suggest (with apologies to rare writers like Bunyan and Defoe and a few others) we have a slogan: LITERARY ENGLISH FROM CAXTON TO US IS AN ARTIFICIAL JARGON OF THE RULING CLASS; WRITTEN ENGLISH BEGINS WITH US; or another slogan: WE ARE REVOLUTIONARY WORKING-CLASS WRITERS; WE HAVE GOT TO MAKE USE OF THE LIVING LANGUAGE OF OUR CLASS; also: ALLUSIVE WRITING IS CLIQUE WRITING: WE ARE NOT A CLIQUE.

Suggestion 3. The middle-class search for serious literature (the 'crisis of ideas') is of course not a separate phenomenon, as the statement rather suggests. It is partly a sign of how deeply the crisis of capitalism even in imperial England is biting directly down into the complacent petty middle-class; it is also partly due to the final complete development of capitalism in book production, which naturally lowers the quality of fiction produced by the popular novelist etc. (hack of the printing and paper industry) and drives the intelligent or honest few who have not crossed to our side into a displeasing cynicism and cleverness. Our task in regard to this middle-class is to organize our destructive criticism of their morals, their religion and their rachitic ethics.

We must take advantage of the worsening position of this middle-class; those of us who write using the bourgeois channels should give earnest attention to this work. But while we do this, and assist the more intelligent and honest members of the class over to our side, we must never fail to maintain Robespierrian suspicion, we must never forget that the present distaste for Fascism and love of 'democracy' among them is with most of them merely a result of the fact that the usual petty middle-class comfort-loving squeamish-ness is more than generally marked in the leading imperialist country, and incidentally makes these folk, except in rare cases, the most unreliable and weak-kneed allies.

(I, 3: 76–7)

From Montagu Slater [January 1935]

I have a minor quarrel with the 'statement of aim.' I agree that the 'crisis of ideas' is a convenient starting point: indeed, it was the actual starting point for very many of us. But like what you call 'the decadence of the past twenty years of English literature,' its importance as a separate phenomenon can be exaggerated. Your period of twenty years narrows the questions. The truth is that capitalism never found literature a comfortable ally: the bourgeoisie blunted the pen point whenever it could (more successfully in capitalist England than in France whereby hangs – critically – an interesting tale). A sense of crisis and decadence has been reflected in literature, as a permanent symptom of capitalism, for 150 years.

There is a passage in the *Communist Manifesto* which expresses indirectly the special discomforts of literature inside capitalism. 'Whenever the bourgeoisie has risen to power it has destroyed all feudal, patriarchal, and idyllic relationships. It has ruthlessly torn asunder the motley feudal ties that bound men to their "natural superiors"; it has left no other bond betwixt man and man but crude self-interest and unfeeling "cash payment." It has drowned pious zeal, chivalrous enthusiasm, and humdrum sentimentalism in the chill waters of selfish calculation. It has degraded personal dignity to the level of exchange value; and in place of countless dearly-bought chartered freedoms, it has set up one solitary unscrupulous freedom – freedom of trade. In a word, it has replaced exploitation veiled in religious and political illusions, by exploitation that is open, unashamed, direct and brutal.'

There is, I think, no question but that the arts are on the whole less fruitful under capitalism than under the conditions capitalism replaced. 'Commodity exchange begins where community life ends,' says Marx in *Capital*. 'In bourgeois society,' says the *Manifesto*, 'capital is independent and has individuality, whereas the living person is dependent and lacks individuality.' Obverse and reverse of the same medal!

And when Capitalism is achieved, when man becomes an atomic unit, 'free,' equal, a voter, and *unreal*, then social relations are no longer between men, but between things, or between commodities: action and passion is between Rolls Royces and macadam roads. Art has lost its subject-matter. This subject-matter – man – can only exist in social relations: and art at last may rediscover him, not in social relations in the older *civilized* sense of the term, but in social battle, in class war, in the war to end the atomic capitalist regime.

In such a statement of position there is, implicitly, I think, a claim that we are *carrying forward* the pre-capitalist assets and the capitalist assets too. But this needs formulating carefully.

'The social productive organisms of ancient days,' says *Capital*, 'were far simpler, enormously more easy to understand, than is bourgeois society; but they were based, either upon the immaturity of the individual human being (who had not yet severed the umbilical cord which, under primitive conditions, unites all members of the human species one with another) or upon direct relations of dominion and subjugation.' In the simplicity of societies is sometimes found the explanation for the attractiveness of their literature. 'The Greeks were normal children,' says Marx in that passage in the *Critique of Political Economy*, where he finds that Greek writing and art 'in certain respects prevail as the standard and model beyond attainment.'[1] And then Marx carries the point further. The old, simple organization of society was 'an outcome of a low grade of the evolution of the productive powers of labour; a grade on which the relations of human beings to one another within the process by which they produced the material necessities of life, and therefore their relations to nature as well, were correspondingly immature. This restrictedness in the world of concrete fact was reflected in the ideal world, in the world of the old natural and folk religions. Such religious reflections of the real world will not disappear until the relations between human beings in their practical everyday life have assumed the aspect of perfectly intelligible and reasonable relations as between man and man, and as between man and nature. The life process of society, this meaning the material process of production, will not lose its veil of mystery until it becomes a process carried on by a free association of producers, under their conscious and purposive control. For this, however, an indispensable requisite is that there should exist a specific material groundwork (or series of material conditions of existence) which can only come into being as the spontaneous outcome of a long and painful process of evolution.'[2] (*Capital*, Chapter I, Section 4: 'The Mystery of the Fetishistic Character of Commodities.')

It is a long quotation but it contains a great deal. My own application is this. Capitalism, and the process of scientific enlightenment which its own greed has forced the bourgeoisie dubiously and grudgingly to permit, has carried us to the point where 'perfectly intelligible and reasonable relations as between man and man, and as between man and nature,' are at last seen to be possible – at the price of the supersession of capitalism. The painful process of evolution and scientific enlightenment has been marked till now by bewildering complexity: the arts have been baffled: and in consequence the cultural legacy of capitalism has been almost exclusively scientific in form. But as we, at any rate, begin to conceive the possibility of intelligible and reasonable relations, we see the possibility of other than scientific expression: maybe the time is coming when mankind goes on from algebraic formula to poem again, re-enacting the Grecian intelligibility 'the standard and model beyond attainment' on another plane.

A final quotation from the *Communist Manifesto* sums the position up. 'In bourgeois society living labour is but a means for increasing the amount of stored labour. In communist society, stored labour is but a means for enlarging, enriching, furthering the existence of the workers. In bourgeois society, therefore, the past rules the present; but in communist society the present rules the past.'

In communist society the present rules the past – or, better, eats, drinks, enjoys, makes use of it. 'All history is contemporary history,' says Croce. But the statement, like the man who made it, stands ambiguously between socialist optimism and fascist fatalism. Let our slogan, then, be that we are going to utilize history (and as writers let us include literature) for the purposes of the class which is going to build socialism.[3]

I read last month's contributions to this discussion with much interest and to give particularity to my generalizations I shall add a comment or two. I think it follows from any statement of the full marxist position that Alec Brown is mistaken when he wants us to turn with him contemptuous backs on 'the vast jellyfish of the petty middle-class.' Unfortunately it is the class to which any professional or semi-professional writer, whether he likes it or not, belongs to. (It is only in the U.S.S.R. that it is in practice possible for writers to turn from their typewriters for six months and take with a sigh of relief a six months spell in a factory.) So, since our aim is to bring writers into the fight under working-class leadership, the jellyfish has a place in our kettle.

Alec Brown is, I think, touching an important point when he demands that 'we should get right down to spoken English in our work.' The speech of the men 'at the hidden foci of production,' workers and technologists, craftsmen and peasants, is the air a live literature must breath.[4] (Incidentally, this contradicts Brown's slogan about 'allusive writing': for nothing could be more allusive than such talk.)

It is in short the strongest argument for a Writers International that it can bring writers into touch with life. ('Life' in this context equals the class struggle – for proof of which vast claim I can only refer readers to the first part of this statement and all issues past and future of the *Left Review*.) If in making such claims our language, as Sherard Vines complains [Professor Sherard Vines contributed to the controversy in the previous number], becomes emotional rather than scientific, let practice and criticism work to amend it: but I would urge Sherard Vines to consider whether opposition to 'every conceivable kind of armed force' is not at this stage, if not the language, certainly the logic of emotionalism.

I recapitulate thus: (1) Literature concerns human relationships. Capitalism destroyed these in their primitive forms, substituting money or commodity relationships. The mere struggle to re-establish free human relationships in a non-mystical, intelligible form is among other things a fight for a better chance for literature.

(2) The working-class is necessarily the political and practical leader of this struggle. This does not mean that we start from scratch a proletarian culture. Among our jobs is that of making the stored-up literary labour of the past usable by the present. In return we can be put in communication with (and write about) real men instead of bourgeois money-bags. But to do so we must step into the cold air of the practical world where we shall find that the fight against 'the rule of commodities' is a fight of actual men against flesh-and-blood enemies armed both with words – and guns.

Notes

1. The difficulty is not in grasping the idea that Greek art and epos are bound up with certain forms of social development. It rather lies in understanding why they still constitute with us a source of aesthetic enjoyment and in certain respects prevail as the standard and model beyond attainment.

    'A man can not become a child again unless he becomes childish. But does he not enjoy the artless ways of the child and must he not strive to reproduce its truth on a higher plane? Is not the character of every epoch revived, perfectly true to nature, in child nature? Why should the social childhood of mankind, where it had obtained its most beautiful development, not exert an eternal charm as an age that will never return? There are ill-bred children and precocious children. Many of the ancient nations belonged to the latter class. The Greeks were normal children.' – *Fragmentary Introduction to the Critique of Political Economy.*

    Marx once named Shakespeare, Aeschylus and Goethe as his favourite poets, Diderot as his favourite prose writer.

2. Some readers will want to seize on the word 'spontaneous' as if to say 'There you are! Marx himself thinks of the revolutionary change in society as something that occurs when the time is ripe, something which our efforts can as little help or hinder as they can help or hinder an express train.' But if there are such objectors and they re-read the quotation, perhaps they will begin to see that *intelligible relations* can only come of active intelligence and intelligent action.

3. This is a very different thing from saying with Alec Brown in the December *Left Review*, 'Written English begins with us.' Fortunately it doesn't.

4. An amusing example of how people of considerable political shrewdness are scared off by the literary power of such speech is to be found in the English translation of a famous passage of Stalin. Stalin warned the imperialists 'to keep their hog-snouts out of our Soviet potato patch,' a powerful and lively image which in all the English translations was suburbanized into 'Keep their hog-snouts out of our Soviet garden.'

    (I, 4: 125–8)

From C. Day Lewis [January 1935]

I believe that the substance and object of this statement are of vital importance to all writers who aim at something more than superficial entertainment. I agree that this Association will be able to do very valuable work in helping such writers to clarify their ideas and thus to present in their writing a more accurate and compelling picture of contemporary society. It is already becoming more evident to serious writers that the prevailing 'consciousness' of the times is a political consciousness, and this is increasingly manifest in their work. Unfortunately, although the old conception of 'pure' art – art as an activity and an existence fundamentally divorced from 'ordinary' life and on a different plane from it – is rapidly losing grip, the effects of this belief still linger in the unconscious mind of the writer and distort his approach to his work. The Association therefore must have as one of its basic objects the building up of a new conception of the nature of literature. It will achieve this by bringing together writers who are convinced of the necessity for this new conception.

Those who realize that revolutionary socialism is the only alternative to the collapse of all that is best in that civilization which great writers have played a prominent part in building – is the channel into which life must run if we are not to have chaos again – will feel bound to use their powers as writers consciously and deliberately to this end. They will not be frightened by the old bogy which threatens the artist with the loss of his 'independence' and 'integrity' if he allows political convictions to mould his work. Nor will they mind being accused of producing 'propaganda' instead of literature. The starting-point of a poem, for instance, is a strong feeling about something: a strong feeling about the state of society is just as legitimate a motive for a poem as any other, and if the poet has an equally strong conviction as to the remedy for this state, the resulting poem is bound to have a propagandist effect and is not in the least likely to be an inferior poem in consequence.

Paragraphs 2 and 3 of your statement seem to me open to criticism. You say that journalism, literature, etc., to-day must be charged with triviality in so far as they do not deal with 'the events and issues that matter': at the same time you speak of 'the decadence of the past twenty years of English literature'! Surely there is a contradiction here. Every serious book is bound to reflect to some degree the outstanding or underlying facts of the contemporary scene, 'the events and issues that matter' – whether the writer is deliberately using them or unconsciously influenced by them: he cannot live in a vacuum. The decadence of recent literature is due to the fact that honest artists have been reflecting the decadence of society: it is not the result of artists shutting their eyes to the most important issues. I am not, of course, objecting to your implied thesis – that literature will inevitably be decadent now unless it is looking towards the birth of a new world – for this is a fundamental of our position. But I feel we should not alienate honest writers, who are at present 'neutral,' by accusing them of supplying 'distraction' and of running away from the issues that matter. It is the business of our Association to clarify these issues for them and to convince them that our method of approach is the right one.

One more small point. Your statement conveys the impression of lumping together journalism, literature and the theatre as equal in point of triviality. This may be correct, generally speaking. But I feel that the mere lumping of them together may be apt to imply, for the neutral reader and writer, that we are disregarding the very different approach which each of them must make to reality. The approach of the text-book and the newspaper article should obviously be direct, that of the novel or play indirect: the latter have to give insight into the causes of events imaginatively through the reaction of society upon the individual or of one individual on another. The tendency of much proletarian art is to use individuals as lay-figures expressive of political ideas instead of depicting them as living agents and instruments of political forces. This distinction between 'ideas' and 'forces' is not, of course, a valid one, but only an erroneous impression conveyed to the reader by a form of art which is still finding its feet. But the fact remains that the imaginative writer who simply uses characters to express a political philosophy will find that he has produced not a novel or a play, but an illustrated text-book. This is common-place and there was obviously not scope in your statement to deal with the different methods of approach of different types of writing. It is, however, perhaps worth while making the point, as writers who are not yet in our movement are inclined to think that we confuse the direct statement of reality-propaganda, with the indirect expression of reality-art; and are inclined to hold aloof from us under the impression that we demand from them only the former. I feel sure our Association can do its best work (*a*) in proving that revolutionary ideas and art are not incompatible and (*b*) in affirming that no one can be a revolutionary writer who has not thoroughly assimilated these ideas by carrying them into practice.

(I, 4: 128–9)

From Lewis Grassic Gibbon

[February 1935]

A great part of the thesis seems to me to propound ideas which are false and projects which are irrelevant.

It is nonsense to say that modern literature is narrowing in 'content'; there was never in the history of English letters such a variety of books on such a variety of subjects, never such continuous display of fit and excellent technique. One need do no more than glance through an issue of *The Times Literary Supplement* to be convinced of this.

To say that the period from 1913 to 1934 is a decadent period is just, if I may say so, bolshevik blah. Neither in fiction, sociological writing, biography (to take only three departments) was there work done half so well in any Victorian or Edwardian period of equal length.

So-called revolutionary statements on decadence (such as that contained in the resolution) seem to me to be inspired by (*a*) misapprehension; (*b*) ignorance; or (*c*) spite.

It is obvious that such revolutionists imagine that modern fiction means only Aldous Huxley, modern drama Noel Coward, modern biography the Lytton Stracheyites, and modern history the half-witted Spenglerites.

So much for misapprehension and ignorance. But the spite is also very real. Not only do hordes of those 'revolutionary' writers never read their contemporaries (they wallow instead, and exclusively, in clumsy translations from the Russian and German) but they hate and denigrate those contemporaries with a quite Biblical uncharitableness and malice. With a little bad Marxian patter and the single adjective 'bourgeois' in their vocabularies they proceed (in the literary pages of the *Daily Worker* and like organs) to such displays of spiteful exhibitionism as warrant the attentions of a psycho-analyst. From their own innate second-rateness they hate and despise good work just as they look upon any measure of success accruing to a book (not written by one of their own intimate circle) with a moronic envy.

Not all revolutionary writers (I am a revolutionary writer) are cretins. But the influence of such delayed adolescents, still in the grip of wishfulfilment dreams, seems to have predominated in the drawing up of this resolution. Capitalist literature, whether we like it or not, is not in decay; capitalist economics have reached the verge of collapse, which is quite a different matter. Towards the culmination of a civilization the arts, so far from decaying, always reach their greatest efflorescence (the veriest tyro student of the historic processes knows this).

That efflorescence is now in being. It is not a decayed and decrepit dinosaur who is the opponent of the real revolutionary writer, but a very healthy and vigorous dragon indeed – so healthy that he can still afford to laugh at the revolutionist. If revolutionary writers believe they can meet in fraternal pow-wows and talk the monster to death by calling it 'bourgeois' and 'decadent' they are living in a clown's paradise.

★ ★ ★

Having said all this in criticism, I'll proceed to a little construction:

First, I'm in favour of a union of revolutionary writers. But this union would

(a) Consist only of those who have done work of definite and recognized literary value (from the revolutionary view-point). It would consist of professional journalists, novelists, historians, and the like, who before admittance would have to *prove* their right to admittance.

(b) Exclude that horde of paragraphists, minor reviewers, ghastly poetasters and all the like amateurs who clog up the machinery of the left wing literary movement.

(c) Set its members, as a first task, to drawing up a detailed and unimpassioned analysis of contemporary literature and the various literary movements.

(d) Be a shock brigade of writers, not a P.S.A. sprawl.

I hate capitalism; all my books are explicit or implicit propaganda. But because I'm a revolutionist I see no reason for gainsaying my own critical judgment – hence this letter!

(I, 5: 179–80)

From Douglas Garman [February 1935]

I believe the chief value of the Writers' International lies in its ability to make clearer the nature of the forces that are disintegrating contemporary society, and by doing so to show that the future of civilization depends on the achievement of Communism. It is, therefore, necessarily an important part of its work to give a precise and cogent meaning to the abused word 'civilization,' which entails, for us particularly, the constant showing up of the pretentious humbug of democratic culture as represented by popular fiction, the film, etc. It is equally important that we should be on the alert to discover the social symptoms of the increasing muddle-headed drift towards imperialist war and to reveal the many insidious developments of Fascism that are taking place quite independently of Mosley and his Blackshirts. These are partly propagandist jobs, but, more importantly for the Writers' International, critical ones. The direct 'encouragement' of imaginative writing should, I think, be quite a secondary concern; though, indirectly, nothing can be of greater service to literature than the clarifying of social issues and the building up of a sound ideology.

In this respect, I agree with Slater's comment that the 'crisis of ideas' referred to in the original statement of aims is not a matter merely of the last twenty years, but has been reflected with varying degrees of intensity in the literature of the last one hundred and fifty. Even the best poetry of that period is characterized by its failure to discover a common denominator between the poetic and the real worlds. Wordsworth realized this to some extent theoretically, and his best work is the result of his realization, but his analysis of the underlying cause did not go deep enough. Much of his poetry might serve as a commentary on Marx's description of the capitalist era in *The Poverty of Philosophy*: 'Lastly, there comes a time when all that men have regarded as inalienable become objects of exchange, of traffic, and can be disposed of. It is the time in which even the things which until then had been communicated, but never exchanged; given, but never sold; acquired, but never bought – virtue, love, opinion, science, conscience, etc. – where all at last enter into commerce. It is the period of general corruption; of universal venality. ...' But Wordsworth did not see forward to men revolting against this tyranny of money and machines. He retreated instead to the dying world of the peasantry, and by attempting to establish there the world of poetry, accentuated the difference between poetry and life.

Later, this flight from reality took another form, though the cause remained the same. As the chaos of capitalism increased, poetry turned even further from the world of actuality and found a temporary refuge in the theory of 'pure poetry.' In this country it never suffered that healthy infusion of the life of streets and cities which invigorated the work of Baudelaire and, through him, a whole generation of French poetry. It is only since the war that English poets, realizing that a belief in 'pure poetry' leads inevitably to a dead end, have begun again to find their subject matter in contemporary life. They are still, however, too often hampered by the absence of any consistent and generally accepted 'world-view,' and are thus obliged to make shift with a personal and idiosyncratic structure of ideas and symbols. To this is due the difficulty and obscurity of much contemporary work.

I cannot, however, agree with the solution implied by Alec Brown's commentary in the December *Left Review*, that we should chuck all existing literature overboard in order to create a real proletarian culture. The criticism once made by Marx of a fraction of the Communist League[1] might well be applied, with but slight alteration, to what he writes: 'While we specially point out the undeveloped nature of the German proletariat to the German workers, you flatter the national feelings and craft prejudices of the German handicraftsman in the crudest way, which is of course more popular. Just as the democrats turned the word *"people"* into a sacred being, so you have done with the word *"proletariat."'* Indeed, Brown's proposed slogan: 'Literary English from Caxton to us is an artificial jargon of the ruling class; written English begins with us,' strikes me as being itself an unfortunate example of jargon. One might as well have told the builders of the Dnieperstroy dam to pay no attention to pre-Soviet science because it is tainted with bourgeois prejudice.

Surely, on the contrary, it is of the greatest importance that we should make the fullest possible use of the literature of the past, so that by reorientating our experience of it to a revolutionary view-point we can make it serve as the basis for a newly vitalized and really contemporary form of expression. We can do this mainly through a fuller understanding of dialectical materialism and by constantly applying Marxist principles – not politically, that is being done elsewhere – but in the more generalized field of social and cultural experience.

I stress the importance of social and literary criticism because that is the weakest side of *Left Review* – and, after all, whatever 'statements of aim' we may make or whatever revolutionary resolutions we may pass, they are little more than hot air unless *Left Review* makes them concrete. Judging by the numbers that have so far appeared, the Editors' aim would seem to be to encourage literary aspirants – sometimes, apparently, for no other reason than that their work has a vaguely revolutionary content – rather than to build up a structure of thought which will make truly revolutionary literature possible. Such important matter as reviews, and even one of the extremely interesting *Revolutionists' Handbooks*, are tucked away in small print, while considerable space is sacrificed to a rather parochial Literary Competition the results of which we never see. It is worth bearing in mind that capitalist publishers are still – though, of course, this may not last for long – willing to publish proletarian and revolutionary fiction; *Fontamara* and *Storm in Shanghai*, both reviewed in the January *Left Review*, are cases in point. But this is largely because it *is* fiction. On the other hand there is no paper in which the cultural and social – as opposed to the mainly political – aspects of Marxist dialectics can be freely discussed, unless *Left Review* provides the opportunity. And my final comment is that, until such discussion is widely and vigorously carried on, proletarian literature is likely to remain a sickly hanger-on of capitalist culture, undistinguished by any more profound change than that its typical hero will be of the 'toiling masses' rather than of the 'pampered bourgeoisie.'

Note

1. Quoted in *Marx-Engels Selected Correspondence*, p. 92.

(I, 5: 180–2)

From Hugh MacDiarmid

[February 1935]

Alec Brown is wrong in what he says about the 'proletarianization of our actual language.' Apart from the fact that to speak of 'getting right down to spoken English' in literary work is a misleading phrase, suggesting an essentially unrealizable objective and depending upon an altogether false equating (almost identifying) of life and literature, the whole attitude means just a kind of 'talking down to the people.' It threatens a short-circuiting of human consciousness and a stereotyping of the cultural disabilities that have been forced upon the working-class by capitalism.

Far more allusive writing (or oral literature) than any contemporary work (except only its remnants in the music halls and in certain strains of working-class talk which are excessively allusive) was not over the heads of working-class people in Elizabethan days, in Gaelic Ireland in the Penal Age, and at many other times, and appeals to a deep-seated human desire, just as the obvious, the over-simplified, the pre-digested 'pap' is abhorrent.

The literature of the future cannot be 'thirled' to limitations that have had their roots in lack of educational opportunity and other methods of mass mutilation. Lenin was right when he insisted upon the full rigour of the word, upon the retention of the entire jargon – the technical terms – of Marxism, and refused to give Russian workers 'Marx-without-tears.' Similarly, in regard to the sciences, the technical terminology is indispensable to an understanding of the points at issue; simplification is falsification. There is no easy way – no short cut – to proletarian culture.

I would add that I am amused to note Alec Brown's insistence on English this and English that, and, similarly, Simon Blumenfeld's quite irrelevant remarks on 'English, the language of forty millions in Britain, millions overseas, and a hundred and twenty millions in America.' Proletarian culture – like every other culture – depends upon considerations of quality, not quantity, and there is no ground whatever for concluding that any better work is likely to be done in a language that hundreds of millions speak and read than in one that is only used by a fraction of a million.

(I, 5: 182)

II.   The Nature of Literature and Art

The most lasting contribution of *Left Review* was the development of Marxist literary theory. However, today, after several decades of abstract theorising, the magnitude of this achievement may not be so obvious. The starting point was a critical approach that rarely offered more than appreciative reflectionism (literature mirrored the content of the world it took as its subject, and it was judged on how closely it reproduced 'objective reality' and the political attitude expressed in the work). Yet within a couple of years the understanding of the demands made on literature by the political situation and the recognition of the complexity of literature's functioning produced literary theory that is still relevant and useful today.

The development was not an even progress, of course. There were statements that assumed the status of theory which displayed an embarrassing gulf between literary understanding and the desire for political change, such as Alec Brown's infamous and often-quoted statement that 'literary English from Caxton to us is an artificial jargon of the ruling class' (see the Writers' International Controversy section, above); but the practical work – the critiques – were generally of a very high standard, although the work they criticised sometimes displayed defects consistent with the stereotype of 'economistic' criticism (see, for example, Edgell Rickword's critique of Philip Henderson's *Literature* in Section IV).

Left Review's development of Marxist literary theory did not come from a mechanical application of Marxism to literature; Marxism offered a perspective that was then fleshed out with specific detail and made into theory by the literary skill of the practitioners. Rickword, for example, was exceptionally sophisticated, powerfully rational and wrote with striking clarity. The rapidity of the theoretical advance was largely due to the link between theory and practice and the shared political purpose that located the criteria for theory in real life. Poetry could be practical – it could transform attitudes. C. Day Lewis wrote, 'It's a long step, of course, from reading poetry to becoming an active revolutionary: but the poetry has in many cases been a first step.' The sense of literature as active and practical provided the basis for defining literature's role, not only in the present crisis but also seen historically.

There was no revolutionary definition of literature from which the contributors to *Left Review* could begin. While a few of them were content with a radical reflectionist notion, others began to open the wider questions of what revolutionary consciousness involves, and then of how literature affects consciousness and in what way it can be politically productive. This was not necessarily reductive. Literature's success in its political job depended on allowing it to function properly as literature, and it required of critics that they recognise its distinctive kind of understanding, the nature of literature as literature. Thus Day Lewis cautions against confusing value as literature with explicit political position:

> First, we must guard against that form of literary sentimentality which would accept any piece of verse evidently written from a revolutionary standpoint and reject everything written from any other angle. The first qualification of a poem is that it should be a good poem – technically good, I mean. A badly-designed, badly-constructed house is not excused by the fact that it was built by a class-conscious architect and workmen. Equally, a poem may have been written by a reactionary bourgeois and yet be a very good poem and of value to the revolutionary; *The Waste Land* is such a one.

The general view was that literature was important as a social product – not just an individual communication – where the reader's experience of it was very much mediated by other cultural factors and personal and social experience. What developed was a sense of literary history shaped by this nature; history was seen as an active process, not just a record, and literature had played a functional role in the development of culture. With the perhaps surprising choice of *The Waste Land* as example, Day Lewis argues that explicit political statement is not at all the same as political effect.

Even though understanding of literature for *Left Review* derived from political practice, from immediate demands, when Alick West reviewed the first five numbers in the hard-line *Labour Monthly* (March 1935), he regretted that it still lacked revolutionary uniformity, that it had 'still something of the character of a "miscellany" instead of the organ of a movement with a perfectly clear aim'. Such 'perfect clarity' was something *Left Review* avoided – not from any lack of political commitment but because the *political* function of literature depended on weighing contradictions in their emotional complexity and the political success of literary criticism depended on treating literature as more than a mirror. Contrary to West, Day Lewis recommends an attitude toward would-be revolutionary writers of 'friendly but severe criticism'. Generally the writers of *Left Review* seemed to take the view that literature was so mediated by other cultural factors and personal and social experience that it could not be subjected meaningfully to a line.

Day Lewis's 'Revolutionaries and Poetry', the first of the articles in this section, opened literary questions in the largest terms, presenting a historical view of poetry and how it developed in relation to function, which was the basis for answering the question of literature's role in the struggle to change society. The range is huge, the knowledge required to support it enormous – and it is perhaps only the actual limitations of the author's knowledge that permitted him to make such sweeping statements. This scope is seminal but was less influential than it might have been, perhaps because it was historically orientated rather than stressing the immediate role of the revolutionary poet.

Although Day Lewis's piece has not been entered in the annals of English criticism, it had significant influence in bringing the anthropological perspective of culture in classic Marxist writing and in Plekhanov's *Art and Social Life* into British Marxist criticism. Christopher Caudwell's theory of culture, articulated little more than a year later and in press when he was killed in Spain in February 1937, owes a great debt to Day Lewis's piece, and it was probably this piece that led him to the perspective in which his own revolutionary theory was produced.

The next article, Douglas Garman's review of *Illusion and Reality*, which appeared two years later, although not relating the book to Day Lewis's article, is connected by Caudwell's dependence on Day Lewis and therefore reasonably is the next selection. Garman, whose reviewing in *Left Review* shows great subtlety of reading and a highly elaborated, complex view of literature's functioning in society, explains Caudwell's complex theory and makes clear that this is a fundamental achievement

of a Marxist literary perspective. He focuses more on Caudwell's integration of contemporary psychological understanding
than on his sense of historical development of function, the
part where his debt to Day Lewis is most evident but also
where he has his least detailed knowledge.

The other piece that can be considered to have made a
theoretical achievement in its own right is Alick West's
discussion of 'The "Poetry" in Poetry', tackling technical
questions of importance and of interest to other major critics
of the day, but seen here also in terms of the social
functioning of poetry. He views the change in technique, the
evolving poetics, against the social structure in a way that
makes clear how social change generates artistic change,
which he manages without a trace of mechanical quality. His
hard-line political position in *Labour Monthly* did not affect
his considerable literary sensitivity.

Eric Gill, in a manner that today would probably be
regarded as theoretically naive, responds to a right-wing attack
on an Artists' International exhibition by saying *all* art is
propaganda – i.e. it asserts values – and that this is art's
function: 'Every artist must be a preacher, a missionary.' In a
second letter he extends the ideas by adding that no art exists
in isolation but only as a part of other activities.

Alick West's reply to Gill seems to be somewhat nit-picking,
concentrating on what appear minor doctrinal differences rather
than accepting Gill's overall sentiments about committed art,
with which West otherwise agrees. He does, however, extend the
theoretical position in saying that the artist's function is 'to
express and change a particular social situation', and that, in
reducing it to craft, Gill conceals its ideological character and, by
implication, restricts its social potential.

Anthony Blunt approaches the problem of realism in art in
a way that is both more concrete and more theoretical than the
argument between West and Gill about craft v. art: he relates
his discussion to the specific characteristics of the art of different historical periods, and at the same time he approaches the
question of 'what is revolutionary art?' through a general consideration of the way in which conventions of representation
relate to class experience. With a language of unusual acces-
sibility, Blunt makes a sophisticated explanation of a complex
and continuing problem (even if his definition of revolutionary
art – 'the art which most closely represents the ideas of the
rising class' – rather glosses over the specific problem). The

piece is short, only about 1,500 words, and while it may not add much to the understanding of art historians, it makes accessible to ordinary readers matters that are fundamental – and remain fundamental – to political thinking about the arts and their social role.

Georgi Dimitrov presents a different kind of material, something that has 'official' status. Dimitrov (as his speech indicates) became an international hero in his defence in the Reichstag trial, and at the time of the speech he was head of the Comintern (the Communist International) and the force behind the Popular Front strategy that the Comintern formally adopted at its Seventh Congress in 1935. His address to a Soviet writers' congress, which *Left Review* reprinted in June 1935, has a clear revolutionary purpose and nobility of proletarian, international solidarity, especially in its oft-quoted conclusion: 'Literature must serve the great revolutionary ideal of millions of workers.' But Dimitrov is a practical politician addressing writers, not a literary expert, and his recognition of the way argument is carried on in literature is at points very limited. Although he warns that 'The man who limits himself to repeating "Long live the revolution," is no revolutionary writer!', his remarks on the excellence of *Don Quixote* suggest a tendency to focus on the literal argument and content rather than the way it is integrated into existing attitudes, conventions, etc., which is the substance of Anthony Blunt's discussion, for example.

The limitations of Dimitrov's view become the limitations of socialist realism. While the goals of educating workers and fostering revolutionary change may have wide, nearly universal adherence on the left, there is considerable difference as to how education and exhortation take place in literature. This problem was certainly recognised by *Left Review* and, although Dimitrov is forcefully praised in the pages of the magazine, most of the contributors seem to feel that what he says has no more than limited relevance to a literary or artistic perspective. On the other hand, it should perhaps be mentioned that Ralph Fox, one of the guiding lights of *Left Review* and a party lecturer on literature until his joining the British Battalion of the International Brigade in Spain, in his best-known work (and the only one still current), *The Novel and the People*, seems to have taken Dimitrov's speech to heart: he echoes Dimitrov's surprise that his heroic resistance in the court at Leipzig has not become a subject for literature and elaborates how it could be made into a novel, and his praise of Cervantes could be seen to echo Dimitrov's.

André Van Gyseghem's 'Letter from Moscow' accepts the same political demands that Dimitrov makes on literature, and he deals with some of the issues raised by Dimitrov, but in a very different way. Van Gyseghem is describing what he sees of Soviet theatre (as the title of the piece suggests); what he writes is theoretical inherently, rather than intended as a theoretical article. He raises the question of 'socialist realism' as a developing technique, not as a shibboleth to straitjacket the theatre; he discusses it in regard, not to 'tractorphilia' but to presenting *individual* psychological problems.

Theatre, as Van Gyseghem describes it, is not just entertainment – it is also work. He takes for granted that art and literature – especially drama – have a function in shaping consciousness, and when that consciousness has changed, so must theatre and its orientation.

What is particularly interesting in Van Gyseghem's piece is that he sees socialist realism taking place in avant-garde theatre. He writes about theatre not as a politician but as a theatrical professional, able to see how a dramatic technique that may superficially appear distant from realism of any sort can be effective in fulfilling functions normally thought of as appropriate to other modes; i.e. in concrete examination he makes clear how educative, attitude-shaping tasks of socialist realism are very well fulfilled by a formalist drama. This is an optimistic view of socialist realism, with a very positive sense of its dramatic and democratic potential.

Revolutionaries and Poetry [July 1935]
C. Day Lewis

The questions are often asked – 'What should be the attitude
of Communists to poetry?' and 'Is poetry of any value to the
revolutionary?' The answer to the first question obviously depends on the answer to the second: the latter is being asked
to-day, not only by workers in the revolutionary movement but
by some of the poets themselves. 'Poetry to-day,' these poets
are inclined to feel, 'has no real contact with the masses': it
therefore has no social value, and we believe that – unless it
has social as well as artistic value – it is not justified. With
two million unemployed in the country and war growing daily
more imminent, surely we are wasting our time singing away
to ourselves in a corner. 'We would be much better employed
doing something practical.' Now this feeling, though understandable, is a sentimental one. The writing of poetry is for
some people their natural activity. We do not expect those who
are good at hewing coal or ploughing or carrying out scientific
research to cease from these activities when they become aware
of world crisis and the necessity for revolution. Here, perhaps,
the ordinary man will interrupt, 'But these are practical, necessary activities: the writing of poetry is a private affair, a kind
of personal luxury.' This argument, though it is a common
one, seems to me sentimental and unhistoric.

In the first place, until about fifty years ago poetry was
accepted as the finest medium through which human feelings
can be expressed. Even when its influence and appeal were
dwindling, it was held in respect. For centuries before this
poetry represented the clearest insight into reality possible to
mankind, and the poet was honoured as the spokesman of
his social group: he expressed what they were feeling both as
a group and as individuals. The historic value of poetry to
the revolutionary would be obvious thus, even if it had not
been underlined by Marx and Lenin. It gives us the clearest
impression of the feelings and aspirations of large groups of

people in the past. It discloses for us emotionally, as science does intellectually, the hidden links in nature. Also, while psychology helps us towards the understanding of our own motives, poetry enables us to feel them more keenly and get them in perspective.

'That is all very well,' the revolutionary may argue; 'I admit the historic value of poetry, and I am prepared to believe that in the past the poet has been a mouthpiece of society and rightly honoured as such. But to-day his function has become obsolete. No one reads poetry; and therefore, even if the poet has the right ideas, he cannot get them across. Anyway, he seems to spend most of his time at present writing stuff I cannot make head or tail of: it doesn't look as if he wanted to be the mouthpiece of anything more than his own complexes.' Let me take the last point first. When poetry is obscure now, it is largely the result of its unpopularity. Until fifty years ago, reading verse was a widespread mental recreation: Shakespeare, for instance, got his poetry across under the guise of entertainment. But the recent growth of newspapers, magazines, cheap fiction, cinemas, radio, etc., has taken the entertainment-value out of poetry. Most people prefer watching Greta Garbo to reading Tennyson. The poet realizes that he is no longer popular: accordingly, he has no incentive to gild his poetry with the stuff of entertainment: he is deprived of that feeling of writing for a wide audience which understood his language; and therefore he begins to write for the tiny circle of people with whom he is in contact, and his poetry sounds to outsiders – what it in fact is – the private language of personal friends. More recently, however, some poets have become dissatisfied with this limited audience and field of expression: they feel strongly the need to communicate with a wider circle: consequently they are trying to simplify their way of saying things, in the hope that this will bring poetry back into popular favour. We shall see, though, that such efforts on the part of individual poets cannot get very far without a revolutionary change in society. Many artists to-day, indeed, are beginning to realize that the full exercise of their powers is only possible under a classless society.

In the meantime, let me take the other argument of the ordinary revolutionary. 'Even if the poet has the right ideas, he cannot get them across'! This I believe to be demonstrably untrue. During the War, Siegfried Sassoon published a volume of poems called *Counter-Attack*: these poems expressed in satire his violent revulsion from all that the war meant. They were a personal expression, as all good poetry is, but they had a considerable influence amongst those numerous intellectuals who had been swept into the war on a tide of Rupert Brooke feeling: I know of several, indeed, whose disillusionment was crystallized by these poems and who became conscious revolutionaries from the moment of reading them. Another point is that a great deal of propaganda can be got across in verse which otherwise would be suppressed. If Sassoon had written his *Counter-Attack* in prose it is highly probable that the book would have been banned and himself imprisoned. But the authorities to-day are inclined to look upon poetry as something that has no bearing on real life, and consequently to overlook what may be contained in it. Again, during the last few years a number of young poets have been expressing their sympathies with Communism in their verse. This has had a very noticeable effect on certain sections of the middle classes, particularly on the students. I know personally over a dozen young men who date their first interest in Marxism from the reading of this kind of poetry: it made them aware of a movement of feeling and action which before they had been blind to or had realized only as something academic, theoretical, unconnected with their own lives. I have had letters from many other intellectuals and not a few workers, both here and in America, which have made it quite clear that this revolutionary poetry has had a real earthquake effect on them – shaken up their ideas and altered the whole map of reality for them. It's a long step, of course, from reading poetry to becoming an active revolutionary: but the poetry has in many cases been a first step.

Granted, then, that poetry can be of value to him, and is therefore something worth criticizing, on what should the Communist base his criticism? I should like to make the following suggestions towards a Marxist critical position. First, we must guard against that form of literary sentimentality which would accept any piece of verse evidently written from a revolutionary standpoint and reject everything written from any other angle. The first qualification of a poem is that it should be a good poem – technically good, I mean. A badly-designed, badly-constructed house is not excused by the fact that it was built by a class-conscious architect and workmen. Equally, a poem may have been written by a reactionary bourgeois and yet be a very good poem and of value to the revolutionary; *The*

Waste Land is such a one. Any good poem, simply because every good poem is a true statement of the poet's feelings, is bound to be of value: it gives us insight into the state of mind of a larger or smaller group of people. Secondly, we must not expect a revolutionary poet to write about nothing but the revolution: he will, presumably, fall in love, admire natural scenery and the movement of machines, suffer personal despairs and exaltations; and he must write about all these. Thirdly, even when he is writing directly from a revolutionary stimulus, we must not expect the result to be the same as our slogans and our pamphlets: we must not look for *direct* propaganda. A poem appeals to the mass through the individual: a slogan, a political speech appeals to the individual through the mass. Poetry is of its nature more personal than 'straight' propaganda: the latter is the heavy artillery, the former is the hand-to-hand fighting. A good poem enters deep into the stronghold of our emotions: if it is written by a good revolutionary, it is bound to have a revolutionary effect on our emotions and therefore to be essentially – though not formally – propaganda. Lastly, what we must ask of our own poets is this: not that they should litter the surface of their poems with red symbols, with hammers and sickles (though these will appear correctly enough in their place); nor with slogans and catchwords (poetry is taking a man aside and talking to him: we do not use slogans and catchwords then; the place for them is the demonstration and the political meeting): nor even that they should be always writing about the class-struggle: what we *have* the right to ask them is that they should thoroughly assimilate Marxism through theory and practical activity; if they have done this, and only if they have done this, will their poetry be revolutionary – blood, flesh and bone. Otherwise, it will remain the old, unregenerate, soft-centred bourgeois, masquerading in a red tie, getting a cheap sensation.

Our attitude, then, towards those poets who declare themselves revolutionaries should be one of friendly but severe criticism. There are not so many of them that we can afford to alienate these by contemptuous references to their bourgeois origin, by charges of 'highbrow-ism,' by approaching them in an atmosphere of personal suspicion. It is their work that our criticism must concentrate on. We must make sure that it is technically good – that it is not imitative, sentimental, insincere, or banal. The poet *is* his poem: the poem is the expression of his real self; and a just criticism of his poem is the only necessary criticism of the poet. At the same time we need to realize that most poets – most artists of any sort – are likely to be 'fellow-travellers.' The artist is more nearly self-contained than any other type of man except the lunatic. The true, original artist is so wholly concentrated on his work that he is often oblivious of economic conditions – his own and those of other people equally: hunger and squalor do actually mean little to him *as an artist*; they do not affect his work to the same degree that they affect the working lives of others. He therefore may have as little incentive to revolutionary activity as the millionaire capitalist. On the other hand he does feel the need to communicate; and it is there that we may make contact with him and enlist his sympathy.

I have said above that 'many artists to-day ... are beginning to realize that the full exercise of their powers is only possible under a classless society.' They wish their work to be understood and appreciated by a great number and diversity of people, not to be the preserve of a few dilettantes. They see that the present system of a society divided into watertight compartments cuts off not only their work but themselves from contact with the masses. They feel that Art which is not rooted in the life of the people must be grievously impoverished and reduced soon to the status of a hot-house plant or a laboratory specimen. Because they need to re-establish contact with the masses, they are impatient of a system which prevents this. If they think on a bit further, they will see the force of the point made by Spender in his recent book, *The Destructive Element*: he says there, the reason why Hitler has been able to stamp out the literary culture of Germany so easily, by getting rid of writers and artists who refused to accept National Socialism, is that this culture had no roots in the life of the masses. Had they had these roots, individual writers might have been exterminated but their culture, their tradition must have remained. This seems to me a very important point, and one that is bound, if properly understood, to bring the 'fellow-travellers' into more active sympathy with the revolutionary movement.

If poetry is to survive as a means of communication, it must become necessary again to people. Necessary, not in the way that bread is necessary, but in the way that an annual holiday in the country is necessary to town-workers: as a refreshment of the emotional life. This may sound to modern ears an extravagant claim. But consider. Poetry is a recreation. It is, first, a perpetual re-creation of language: the poet must have an unusually sensitive ear for words; he listens to the idiom of his age and heightens it into a poetical language. He is the scientist of words; his experiments with them depend for their success on a hair's-breadth accuracy: he is perpetually seeking new combinations of them, as a scientist seeks new chemical combinations. In a period such as the present, when language suffers from exhaustion and from the feverish delirium of the yellow press, this function of the poet is of particular importance. But poetry is more than a recreation, a refreshment of language. It is also a refreshment of the emotional life. What is the instinct which drives people out into the country as often as their economic conditions permit it? We may talk contemptuously about 'escape' and 'nostalgia.' But such words simply shatter themselves on the hard fact. There can be no doubt that it is the instinct to get back to one's roots. For millions of years man lived on and by the land: we are still exiles in the city. The urge that drives us into the country is the desire to return for refreshment to the springs of human life. Well now, it is the same thing with poetry. Poetry was for centuries bound up with the economics of primitive life. The successful hunt, the terror of natural phenomena – earthquake, hurricane, eclipse, the hopes and fears for the harvest, the horror of barren winter and the delight in spring's fertility – all these were expressed by primitive man rhythmically, in dancing and poetry. They were a release of emotion, of directed emotion; and that release meant, like the bursting of a thunder-cloud, refreshment in the end. Poetry was a necessary activity of primitive life. We still find the most vivid, poetical use of language amongst peasants. Now these emotions, based on the fear of cold and hunger, are as keen to-day as they were ten thousand years ago: they have grown a little more complex through the increased complexity of economic conditions: but their sources are the same. Poetry was one of the chief instruments through which primitive man, by expressing his emotions, gained strength to fight against the economic conditions which gave rise to those emotions. It is bound up therefore with our emotional life, and there seems no reason to suppose that it is less necessary to us than it was to our early ancestors.

But there is one important distinction. Most of us to-day live in towns and it is likely that the civilization of the future will be more and more an urban one. Now just as the rise of nineteenth-century capitalism produced the proletariat, a new class of workers which must finally supersede its creator, so the new economic environment of town-civilization must throw up a new class of poets to express the changed emotional conditions. The stage is set for the entrance of the proletarian poet. It is true that bourgeois poets of recent years have drawn their material more and more from town life. But they have been writing from *outside* this life: they are not, and cannot be, the voice out of the heart of the machine. Their verse has expressed, more often than not, a horror of, a desire to escape from, the realities of this new form of life. Even when they are sympathetic towards it and aware of its potentialities, the system of society prevents them from making more than surface contact with it. On the other hand, there is as yet practically no proletarian poetry in England: while in America, though many proletarians are now writing in verse, little first-rate poetry has been produced by them.

What are the difficulties for the proletarian poet? First, he has to make use of an alien tradition. The tradition of poetry for the last hundred years has been developed by a dominating class, the bourgeois. Until the domination of that class is ended, the writer has to make the best of its tradition. A tradition cannot be created independently of the social framework. Not even when the social revolution has taken place can we expect the immediate appearance of a new way of writing: a new tradition does not arrive by virgin birth – it must be worked painfully out of the body of the old. His second difficulty is that tradition in poetry affects the material no less than the material affects the technique. The worker poet at present has to write in a tradition not built for the material he wishes to put into it. What are these new things he wants to bring into poetry? Indignation at the conditions under which he is compelled to live; the feeling of solidarity with his own class and the conviction that he must be a spokesman of that class; the whole range of material data, altered values, and changed emotional stresses which his environment offers him. But, because tradition in poetry affects the material, he has much greater difficulty than the sympathetic bourgeois poet, although the latter feels these things far less strongly and directly, in putting them into the medium of verse. He has to work in an alien tradition – to put new wine into old bottles. His third problem is this. It has been in the interests of capitalism to keep the workers inarticulate. Art, because it speaks directly to the emotions, has always been potentially a revolutionary force. Thus capitalism, as it has given the workers the leavings of its economic production, has tended also to offer them the dregs of its artistic production. As the structure of capitalism has crumbled and the revolutionary situation grown more acute, an ever-increasing flood of false art has been turned upon the workers – the gutter-press newspapers, dope-fiction, sentimental and unreal films. The effect of this has been to weaken the workers' responses to the emotional effect of genuine art. Inoculated with false literature, they find it more difficult to catch the infection of vital and revolutionary literature. In consequence, the worker poet will find himself, like the bourgeois poet to-day, influencing at first only a few of his fellows.

But he has no reason to despair. If his work is true poetry, it will do more than a hundred Boards of Education and culture-fanatics to re-establish art as a vital force; and, if he is a real revolutionary, it will be a revolutionary force too. Let him not think of poetry as a mystery whose secret is held only by the educated bourgeois. If the writing of poetry is his natural activity (and he will soon find that out), all he needs is an English dictionary and a thorough soaking in the English poets. After that, it is a matter of compelling an alien tradition into his own service, just as the U.S.S.R. pressed the industrial technique of capitalist Europe into the service of Socialism. He has a magnificent opportunity before him. He stands inside the workers: he can see at first hand and feel immediately a world which has been to literature so far Terra Incognita. To speak to the workers and for the workers he does not need, as bourgeois poets do, to learn a new tongue: he has only to make poetry of what is his native language.

> ... Sirs, you are that world
> Shall make a new world and be all the world.

(I, 10: 397–402)

Testament of a Revolutionary
(Christopher St. John Sprigg)

[July 1937]

Douglas Garman

It is important to stress the fact that *Illusion and Reality*[1] is the work of a revolutionary. I say this not merely because Sprigg*
was killed in Spain fighting against Fascism, nor because he wrote as a Marxist. Both these facts must be borne in mind. But what makes it specifically revolutionary is the way in which Sprigg apprehended Marxism, firstly as an essentially dynamic view of life, capable not only of explaining but of changing it; and secondly, as a consistent method, applicable to all functions of living, all modes of knowledge. He is therefore at the opposite pole to all those writers who set out from the assumption that art is a separate, isolated function to be discussed only in terms of itself. For him it is a force which, far from being static and subject to immutable aesthetic laws, is constantly changing and being changed by life, by social activity. As he says in the *Introduction*, 'We reject from the outset any limitation to purely aesthetic categories.'

This view of art as social activity and thus, ultimately, as a product of economic conditions, permeates his book. At each stage of his argument, and whatever the subject that argument leads him to discuss, the criterion by which he tests the validity of his conclusions is whether it is consistent with the unity of theory and practice. Such consistency of outlook is in itself distinctive in an age given over to jittering eclecticism and will

---

* Sprigg wrote aeronautics books and crime novels under his own name. For his poetry, his 'serious' novel and his critical work he used the name Caudwell.

59

probably prove a bar to its acceptance by conventional literary critics. Even a would-be Marxist such as Philip Henderson fails to understand its significance, and in a peculiarly inept review in the *Spectator* mistakes its profundity for 'an intricate elaboration of the obvious.' Yet it is precisely this consistency of wealth of knowledge which, far from diverting the attention, serves continually to deepen and strengthen his argument.

Clearly, then, his book is not just another essay in aesthetic appreciation. It is an attempt to give a scientific account of the origin of poetry, to trace its gradual modifications, and then to state the problems it must solve if it is to survive. It is his central thesis that the source of poetry – and by implication of all artistic activity – is to be found in the world of illusion which, as a result of the conflict between man's instinctive, biological desires and the necessity imposed on those desires by conscious social activity, he projects upon reality. These are the illusion and reality to which his title refers, and one could wish that he had chosen another pair of words to express this relation of opposites. For on the face of it it might appear that he conceived of reality as something exclusive of illusion, a dualistic, idealistic conception the very reverse of what he intends. To make his meaning clear he is continually obliged to qualify reality, but even so the qualification is not entirely satisfactory. 'What in fact is the emotional complex of tribal poetry? Is it material reality or completely ideal illusion?' he asks. And the answer is: 'It is neither. It is *social* reality.'

But if his terminology is confused, his meaning is nevertheless clear. By reality, or, as he sometimes calls it, 'external reality,' he means the objective world, and by illusion the sphere of subjective desires and hopes, the individual 'I.' But these two fields of experience, far from being exclusive, are in a continually changing relationship of which art is an expression. Since the ultimate source of all poetry is 'illusion,' it has this constant characteristic. But because the nature of that illusion is determined by the variable objective conditions of which it is a projection, poetry itself changes as these conditions are transformed by economic development. In primitive authors this illusory world is undifferentiated and so finds expression equally in mythology and poetry. But when as a result of the division of labour society begins to split into classes 'religion and art cease to be the collective product of the tribe, and become the product of the ruling class.' Mythology continues to exist as an undergrowth of superstition and legend, but the highest consciousness of society, centred in the dominant class, is expressed in religion and art. Gradually, however, as religion ceases to provide an adequate explanation of reality, it becomes, in the hands of the rulers, merely an instrument used consciously in support of authority. It loses its approach that enables Sprigg to bring to his central theme a living quality and ossifies into dogma, and the function of expressing illusion devolves upon poetry. At such periods, as may be seen by reference to the Elizabethan age, poetry flourished. But though the form that poetry takes must continually be modified in order that it may adapt itself to the changing social relations, its function remains substantially the same. 'Not poetry's abstract statement – its content of facts, but its dynamic role in society – its content of collective emotion is therefore poetry's *truth*.'

It is impossible, however, in a few pages to do justice to the scope and brilliance of the argument, or to follow out its application to modern, i.e. post-feudal, or capitalist, poetry. It must suffice to say that the problem which he finds to be central to this period in life as in art is that of freedom. This is the substance of the 'bourgeois illusion,' the source of its poetry. But 'freedom itself is not a state, it is a specific struggle with nature ... the very act of living and behaving like a man in a certain state of society.' So long, therefore, as society remained at a level of economic development at which the bourgeoisie was unfree, its illusion retains a vital and energising meaning; and its poetry was vigorously alive because it was expressing that illusion. Gradually, however, with man's progressive conquest of nature, the nature of freedom has changed – 'the productive forces released by capitalism have developed to a stage where they are no longer compatible with the limitations which engendered them.' If poetry, therefore, is to retain its vitality, its significance as a social force, it is necessary for it to tear itself away from the 'bourgeois illusion.' Yet so long as we remain subject to bourgeois ideology, as long as we reject the possibility of achieving the new and higher form of society that objective conditions make possible, we cannot do this, and in consequence art, progressively divorced from social reality, becomes increasingly devitalised.

This is the crisis which confronts poetry to-day. In examining it and the conditions necessary for its solution, Sprigg turns to the consideration of the specifically modern characteristics of poetry. Having, in a chapter called *The World and*

the 'I,' given a vivid exposition of the subject-object relationship as it is resolved by dialectical materialism, he proceeds
to criticise the philosophical confusion underlying psycho-
analytic theory. This I believe to be the most masterly
account that has yet been given by a Marxist of modern
analytical psychology. It enables him to separate from much
that is fallacious its positive content, which he is then able
to apply constructively in a chapter called *Poetry's Dreamwork*,
to his central theme. Reverting to his earlier argument, he
points out that by 'freedom' the psychoanalyst means freedom
of the instincts, but as he cogently adds, 'the instincts,
unadapted by society, are blind and therefore unfree.... Man's
freedom is obtained by association, which makes it possible
for him to acquire mastery over Nature through becoming
actively conscious of its necessity and his own.' He thus
differentiates sharply, and conclusively, between the 'free'
association of dream and the directed feeling of poetry. 'The
neurotic is deluded because the complex is in his unconscious; he is unfree. The artist is only illuded because the
complex is in his conscious; he is free.'

Finally, in a chapter written with the eloquence of profound
thought passionately experienced, he sums up his argument
and expresses his belief in the future, not only of poetry but
also of society. 'All art,' he writes, 'is conditioned by the conception of freedom which rules in the society that produces it;
art is a mode of freedom... . In bourgeois art man is conscious
of the necessity of outer reality but not of his own, because he
is unconscious of the society that makes him what he is. He is
only a half-man. Communist poetry will be complete, because
it will be man conscious of his own necessity as well as that of
outer reality.' That so inspiring and confident an utterance
should have proved to be Sprigg's testament, brings home to
us the full tragedy of his death.

Notes

1. *Illusion and Reality*, by Christopher Caudwell. *Macmillan:* 18s.

(III, 6: 352–4)

The 'Poetry' in Poetry [April 1937]

Alick West

The arrival of English literature and criticism at a turning point [is] indicated by a remark of Sidney in *An Apology for Poetry*. Speaking of Spenser's *Shepheards' Calendar*, he says that there is a great deal of poetry in it.

There is a new sense in the word here. Hitherto poetry had been used to designate verse in opposition to prose. According to this old use, the whole of the *Shepheards' Calendar* is poetry; in this new sense, there is more or less poetry in the poetry. What is this new poetry?

Sidney does not give any examples, and we must therefore turn to the literature itself. We cannot be certain of finding out what Sidney had in mind; but we may obtain light on why his remark is felt to be highly expressive.

Instead of the *Shepheards' Calendar*, which was the immediate and probably only the accidental occasion of Sidney's criticism, it will be more convenient in a short article to take Spenser's *Prothalamion*.

The first verse of the poem runs as follows:

Calm was the day, and through the trembling air
Sweet-breathing Zephyrus did softly play
A gentle spirit, that lightly did delay
Hot Titan's beams, which then did glister fair;
When I (whom sullen care,
Through discontent of my long fruitless stay
In prince's court, and expectation vain
Of idle hopes, which still do fly away,
Like empty shadows, did afflict my brain)
Walk'd forth to ease my pain
Along the shore of silver-streaming Thames;
Whose rutty bank, the which his river hems,
Was painted all with variable flowers,

And all the meads adorn'd with dainty gems
Fit to deck maidens' bowers,
And crown their paramours
Against the bridal day, which is not long:
Sweet Thames! run softly, till I end my song.

Even from this verse, and still more from the whole poem, a peculiar difference of quality may be felt between the 'I' in the verse and the 'I' in the refrain – Sweet Thames! run softly, till I end my song – which is repeated at the end of each of the ten verses.

In the verse itself (and again more strongly in a later verse, where Spenser complains of having been deprived of his patron's help) the 'I' refers to Spenser in his own person, discontented with his experiences in society and feeling that he has no place in it. To use a word which hides a difficulty, it has a 'personal' quality.

In the refrain, however, the tone of the 'I' is different, and the difference is felt more with each repetition. This is not Spenser, as a solitary, discontented man, taking his cares out into the open air. The song which he has to sing to the flowing of the Thames is not that of his social disappointments. It is the marriage song of two brides and their bridegrooms, for whose wedding the *Prothalamion* is composed. Spenser is not writing now as a person wandering aimlessly by the river; he has the special function of singing the marriage song within a social group.

The 'I' of the poem, therefore, has two tones in it: the personal tone of Spenser, conscious of his lack of any congenial social activity; the less personal tone of Spenser taking a part in a marriage ceremony.

The one tone affects the other. The personal tone becomes more impersonal, the impersonal more personal. But the 'I' of the complete poem is neither wholly the one nor wholly the other. It is indeterminately between the more 'individual' and the more 'social' Spenser.

The significance of this becomes clearer when we notice that it is particularly the 'I' of the verse which is more personal, the 'I' of the refrain which is less so; and not the other way round. This summarises an historical process.

There seems to be little doubt that in the development of poetry the refrain comes first. The verse grows out of the refrain; the refrain is not suddenly tacked on to an already developed verse, which the modern habit of printing refrains as 'etc.' might make us believe. The earliest form of the refrain, and of poetry at all, seems to have been the continuous, repeated singing of one or two words, accompanied with dancing, by a group. Its meaning was a repeated assertion of the social existence and power of the group; it was the continuous shouting of a slogan of solidarity.

The verse develops out of the refrain as the social existence of the community becomes more complex. The activity of its members becomes differentiated; while the refrain is still kept, particular and differing actions are performed, as the group, or individual members of it, sing and dance and perform each new verse.

Thus the reason why in Spenser's poem the more impersonal tone belongs to the 'I' of the refrain, the more personal to the 'I' of the verse, is in this historical development: the refrain is the expression of a social group in its collective activity, the verse of the differentiation of its members in that activity. The contrast between the 'impersonal' and the 'personal' tone reflects the movement of society from collective communal activity to a form of organisation when the activity of its members becomes more individualised.

In early English poetry, at the time when 'poetry' simply meant 'composed in verse,' the relation to one another of verse and refrain was the relation of that which changes and moves (the verse) to that which is repeated (the refrain). Though there is, I think, a dialectical conflict in this relation, it has not got this peculiar tone of the relation of the 'I' of the refrain to the 'I' of the verse in Spenser's *Prothalamion*.

Moreover, there is something similar in the structure of the poem itself. There is a kind of doubling of planes, which brings into the poem as a whole a polarity resembling that in the 'I.'

The poem is intended to be sung and danced at the marriage ceremony for which it was composed. Probably one or two singers would sing the verses, and a chorus would sing the refrain, either at the end of each verse, or possibly as a burden accompanying it. That is, the manner of performance for which the poem was intended resembles that communal singing of the refrain out of which poetry developed; it is a continuation of poetry in its earliest form.

Further, the content of the poem itself describes, in classicised mythological form, what is essentially its own historical origin. A band of nymphs beside the Thames see two swans floating down the river. They gather flowers in honour of the birds. Two of the nymphs sing to them, while the others bear 'the undersong.' The scene is a 'literary' description of poetry as it was originally sung and acted.

But not only are the nymphs, with their greenish hair, vague compared with the real village singers. The whole scene is shifted on to another plane. It is only *described*. And the quality of the description contradicts in a sense what is described. It is shown through the vision and the mood of Spenser, in the more personal quality of the 'I' who walks in a mood of depression beside the river. The collective singing and dancing, of which there were originally no spectators but only participants, is now perceived in the middle distance, as it were, through the mood of an individual in the foreground who feels himself outcast from social activity.

This peculiar relation between the poem as intended for singing and dancing at a marriage, its mythological description of the early forms of such performances of poetry, and, in contrast, the detachment of the individual spectator through whose feelings the scene is witnessed – this parallels the relation between the personal and the impersonal 'I.'

The poem itself also has two tones: that of a song composed for a marriage feast, and that of a poem expressing Spenser's melancholy at having no part in society. Again, the two tones affect one another: the marriage song acquires a personal note; but the personal note is generalised in the marriage song. The poem is neither wholly marriage song, nor wholly personal expression. Like the 'I,' it is indeterminately between the more 'individual' and the more 'social' Spenser.

This indeterminateness and conflict of relationship between the 'I' of the verse and the 'I' of the refrain, between 'personal' and 'impersonal,' between the poet as someone fulfilling a definite social function and as someone feeling he is without a definite social function to fulfil, between the poem as a song for a particular social occasion and as an expression of Spenser's feeling of being banished from all social occasions – this seems to me the basis of the new 'poetry' in poetry observed by Sidney.

The dominance of this quality in English poetry from the rise until the decay of capitalism is not accidental. The fundamental mood, of which it is the expression, is the result of the character of capitalism.

The ruling ideas being the ideas of the ruling class, the poet during the rise and prime of capitalism necessarily thinks and feels in terms of capitalist ideology. But capitalism is, as Marx says, unfavourable to literature. Even though literature attained under capitalism, and through capitalism, added powers of observation and expression, yet at the same time it was frustrated. For capitalism is concerned with the quantity of exchange-value in the commodity, not with the quality of its use-value; and it operates through the anarchy of free competition. In both these aspects it is hostile to literature. Literature is concerned above all with the quality of life; and it was not when they were in an anarchy of competition that men and women created poetry, but when they sang together at their work, at their dances, religious rites and festivals. The very fact of rhythm – not as a mere idea, but as the rhythm of human bodies singing and dancing together – is opposed to the anarchy of capitalism, to its abstract work and its abstract value.

Poets under capitalism are thus compelled on the one hand to use terms of thought in which, however indirectly, these characteristics of capitalism are active. As poets, using rhythmical language in a particular way, they are equally compelled to think and feel and speak and sing in a manner opposed to capitalism; for they are necessarily saying something about the quality of life, which capitalism is indifferent to; and they are saying it in forms which are derived, not from the anarchy of competition, but from collective activity; and which demand collective response and performance if the poetry is to come to its full life. Capitalism cannot put such use of language to any profit, except by degrading it to superficiality – the only poet recognised by capitalism is the Poet Laureate. The poet under capitalism has no function, but at the same time is called upon to misuse his poetic power for a contradictory purpose – the expression in poetry of a social order inimical to poetry. The poet has nothing to do, and the nothing is a contradiction.

This is what underlies the indeterminateness and conflict in Spenser's *Prothalamion* between the 'I' of the refrain and of the verse and in the poem as a whole. He is continuing under changed conditions that collective activity from which poetry developed; but at the same time he can only do so by describing it from the outside, as an isolated, detached individual; for as a poet under rising capitalism he is being cut off from all such collective activity.

This contradiction, and the consequent indeterminateness of

standpoint between the more 'social' and the more 'individual,' need not appear in such an outward form as the difference in tone between the 'I' of the refrain and of the verse in Spenser's poem. It is already inherent in the very attempt by a poet to express a feeling of social isolation in a form which originates from, implies and demands collective activity and response, as even free verse does. And this, in one variation or other, is the poets' main endeavour from Spenser's time till the rise of Socialism (and later, for 'poetry' has lagged behind).

The peculiar indefiniteness resulting from this contradiction seems to be one of the important qualities of the new 'poetry' in poetry. Connected with it is the attempt of the poet to compensate for his indeterminateness in the poem as a whole by being determinedly poetical in particulars; and also to minimise the conflict by keeping his poems short. With the development of capitalism, poetry pays increasing attention to detail. It endeavours, as Keats advised Shelley, to load every rift with poetic ore. The first line of Spenser's poem is an example:

Calm was the day, and through the trembling air ...

'Trembling,' coming after 'calm,' has this new 'poetical' quality. The word becomes a poem in itself. But the poem as a whole, for which capitalism has no use, tends to disintegrate into 'poetical' phrases.

The older poems were not poems of phrases. Nor are the new ones.

(III, 3: 164–8)

Eric Gill on Art and Propaganda

[June 1935]

'Marxism is in the air. Under a semblance of concern for world peace, Marxism attempts to enlist all peace-lovers in its bogus "anti-war" organizations. ... Under the semblance of concern for democratic drama and cinema, Marxist propaganda ... is being launched in Europe, England and America. Under cover of a society calling itself the "Artists' International" Marxism has recently invaded the domain of art. ...

'Let there be no mistake about this British section of the so-called Artists' International. It is neither British nor International; nor is it primarily concerned with art.'

This is from an article printed in 'The Catholic Herald' October 27th, 1934, and inspired by the first Artists' International exhibition in London. A correspondence which followed drew from Eric Gill, one of the exhibitors, two letters setting forth a point of view which is put on record as showing currents of thought among English intellectuals which ought not to be ignored by Left Review.

Sir, – As one of the exhibitors at the exhibition of pictures arranged by the society called the Artists' International, held in London recently, you will perhaps allow me to comment upon the remarks of your contributor, G. M. Godden.

I visited the exhibition rather expecting to find many 'anti-God' paintings, as I had been told I should do, but in half an hour's walk round I could see none. All I saw were various works depicting the hardships of the proletariat, the brutality of the police, the display of armed forces against street orators, starving children, and slum conditions generally. There were also a few works in the vein of Van Gogh's famous 'Yellow Chair,' that is to say, works depicting simple workmen and scenes of working life.

It was not a big exhibition. It was not held in a fashionable quarter. It might be described as a pathetic affair compared with the exhibitions of what your contributor doubtless calls 'Art' in fashionable West End galleries and art dealers' shops.

Suppose it to be true that the Artists' International is primarily concerned to propagate Communism; even so, there was nothing, in the terms under which we exhibited, which made it obligatory. And there was nothing to hinder any Catholic artist from showing that he could stand up for social justice as well as any Marxian.

So much for that aspect of the affair. But I am less concerned to defend the exhibition than to defend the principle governing it. Your contributor says that the exhibition was 'neither British nor international nor primarily concerned with art.' Further on she says that the Union was not created 'to promote good art but as a section of the army of propagandists.' Further, she quotes Lenin's saying that 'art must serve propaganda,' and, describing a discussion which took place at the exhibition, she says: 'Speakers denounced the present English social system and the Sedition Bill – subjects familiar to Communist speakers but unexpected in a course of addresses connected with an exhibition of art.'

Now what, may I ask, is this extraordinary thing called art if it is not propaganda or at the service of propaganda? What are the sculptures on the medieval cathedrals and in modern churches but propaganda? What are the effigies of eminent politicians in Westminster Abbey and Parliament Square if they are not propaganda for the values and politics upheld by famous statesmen? What is the Royal Academy exhibition but propaganda for the bourgeois culture of modern England; just as Van Gogh's 'Yellow Chair' is propaganda for the values of simple people and simple things?

Art which is not propaganda is simply aesthetics and is consequently entirely the affair of cultured connoisseurs. It is a studio affair, nothing to do with the common life of men and women, a means of 'escape.' Art in the studio becomes simply 'self-expression,' and that becomes simply self-worship. Charity, the love of God and your neighbour, which, here below, every work of man must exhibit, is lost. If you say art is nothing to do with propaganda, you are saying that it has nothing to do with religion – that it is simply a psychological dope, a sort of cultured drug traffic. I, at any rate, have no use for it. For me, all art is propaganda; and it is high time that modern art became propaganda for social justice instead of propaganda for the flatulent and decadent ideals of bourgeois Capitalism.

Every artist must be a preacher, a missionary. But it does not follow that he should make up his own sermons. What is wanted is precisely what Lenin said, with this difference: that, as Catholics, we are serving not the propaganda of Marxian materialism but the propaganda of the Kingdom of God and his justice. –

Yours, etc., *Eric Gill.*

Sir, – With reference to the letter of Mr. Edward Walters in your issue of December 29th, may I again protest against the implications in his sentence: 'The "Artists' International" exhibition was primarily concerned with communist propaganda and only secondarily with art'? Why do people persist in writing about art as though it were an activity performed *in vacuo*? (as who should say: 'I've eaten my breakfast, polished my boots, written an article on sunsets, and now I'm going to do some art'). Such and such, they say, is 'propaganda,' but not art. Such and such is 'religion,' but not art. An exhibition of gas cookers is not art, it is 'commerce' – and so on, and if you ask: What then is art? no two people give you the same answer. The truth is that there is no such thing. It's like the Snark – a Boojum. It's like the emperor's new clothes – not really there at all. There are, in fact, as many arts as there are human activities, but no such thing as art by itself.

All things made are works of art – from the art of stirring the Christmas pudding to the art of M. Picasso who stirs our aesthetic sensibilities; from the making of gas cookers which will cook to making houses for the Blessed Sacrament (i.e. cathedrals and such) – and painting pictures which stir us to rebel against capitalist exploitation is as much art, ART, as painting Madonnas to stir us to the love of God.

Sir, what I protest against is not your correspondent's objection to Communism but the frightful notion that people who make things are not concerned with propaganda – that when I make a statue of Saint Isidore it is bought by some connoisseur not because he loves the saint but because he likes the shape of my sculpture – that in Giotto's paintings of Saint Francis it is not Saint Francis who matters most but something called 'plastic form.' And if a statue means anything the connoisseurs won't like it – they say it's propaganda. They don't want to be disturbed in their complacency, they prefer what Mr. Aldous Huxley calls 'the feelies.' And our painters and sculptors accept this dope; they are proud to be free from any taint of propaganda, they talk about 'pure art.'

Can we not agree that pictures painted under the inspiration of Communism are as much 'art' as pictures painted under the inspiration of Christianity – that a picture painted in the service of religion (any religion) is no less a work of art than one painted simply to entertain? God forbid that all painters should start inventing new religions; but may God equally forbid the continuance of the notion that art has nothing to do with anything but aesthetics.

Yours, etc. *Eric Gill.*

(I, 9: 341–2)

A Reply to Eric Gill [July 1935]
Alick West

The *Left Review* published last month two letters by Eric Gill, in which he attacked the people who write about art 'as though it were an activity performed *in vacuo*.' They are our enemies too.

The *Left Review*, however, cannot take Eric Gill's line; for these reasons.

Eric Gill says that instead of conceiving art as an isolated activity we must see it as propaganda for the Kingdom of God. We will leave the question of God for a moment, since it may be objected that the word is only something accidental. For Eric Gill apparently does not insist on God. He regards both 'the inspiration of Communism' and 'the inspiration of Christianity' as a possible source of art, he seems to class both the Communist and the Catholic together as the preachers who therefore can be artists, in opposition to the aesthete who dopes himself with self-worship. It might therefore be felt that Eric Gill only means that art must be the expression of collective emotion in protest against bourgeois exploitation and individualism.

Such a general statement, however, is in itself valueless. If in its application it includes Catholicism and Communism as sources of the necessary collective emotion, it becomes wrong and harmful. Catholicism and Communism can only be grouped together in terms of a vague, formalistic sentimentality which sees both as expressions of group feeling opposed to individualistic self-worship. This view makes the emotion the primary reality. Eric Gill takes up the idealistic position that it is a group emotion in the artist that is the basis of art, not the concrete social activity outside the artist, in which he takes part.

Further, the fact that a man can only class Communism and Catholicism together, as Eric Gill does, by concentrating all the time on the supposedly common emotions as the vital reality, means that in order to guard this idealistic position he must shut his eyes to the irreconcilable differences of the corresponding social action. When Eric Gill says that he, as Catholic, can protest against social injustice as well as any Marxian, he must forget, as Catholic, that the Holy Roman Catholic and Apostolic Church has declared Socialism incompatible with Catholic piety; or he must imagine that there is some other force that can overthrow capitalism besides the proletariat. In either case he must blind himself to the facts, which, with all the mental repressions and conflicts necessary to hold such a contradictory position, is fatal to good artistic work. If an artist is thus forced to ignore the facts, he must return to the aesthetic self-worship which Eric Gill attacks, having no material to draw on except his own emotion. Propaganda against capitalism, in the name only of religious charity, cannot rescue art from the effects of capitalism; for it means turning away from the particular social relations, which are the artist's material. And it will fail as propaganda, for propaganda can only mobilize the masses if it is based on their particular situation.

The other main weakness in Eric Gill's standpoint is similar. He says that making gas-stoves which will cook is as much art as painting pictures. This also is an attractive idea, apparently bringing art back to earth again: art is a craft like any other, and the good artist is the man who is good at his job. If one could conceive society as absolutely stable, this idea would be true. But under existing conditions a man who makes a gas-stove, does not only create a gas-stove, but also a commodity. Object of use and object of exchange at one and the same time, the gas-stove dances and stands on its head like Marx's table. The difference between art and craft is that in art these antics are visible. Although the gas companies said 'Celebrate the Jubilee with Gas,' yet in the pop when the match is applied to the burner not even the sharpest ear can hear 'God Save the King'; in other words, no one can see in a gas-stove the social relations in which it was manufactured. But the social relations in which a work of art is created and the part played by the artist in carrying them on and changing them, can be and are felt in the work of art. To express and change a particular social situation is the life of art; Eric Gill kills art by degrading it to the relatively inexpressive craft. The reason is again his emotional formalism. His desire to believe in religious feeling as the basis of art, compels him to put the particular social relations out of his own mind, and he therefore says that the craft which does not express them, is also art, meaning not a human activity like any other, or he would not be so emphatic about it, but – art.

Thus in his conception of religious feeling as the basis of art, and of art itself as craft, Eric Gill cuts out the existing social relations. But he must inevitably express them and his relation to them somehow.

He does so through his phrase 'the Kingdom of God.' The words are not accidental. The use of them means that his conception of social relations is the necessary counterpart to the refusal to see them materialistically. He conceives them as the ruling classes of the past centuries have declared they must be conceived – as a higher spiritual mysterious unity, whose will is divine. And it is its will – the will of this class – that at the present moment artists should be humble craftsmen, serving God, serving the propaganda that disguises the existing social relations in the interests of capitalism, instead of seeing and taking part in the class war on the side of the workers.

Because of these elements in his thought Eric Gill cannot stand up against social injustice as well as a Marxian, though we believe he wants to.

(I, 10: 410–11)

The 'Realism' Quarrel [April 1937]
Anthony Blunt

The problem that most deeply concerns artists of to-day is that of realism. For most of the last thirty years no painter or sculptor of any sensibility has thought of the possibility that the first aim of his art might be the rendering of the outside world. The concern of the artist was either to express himself or to create a particular kind of formal pattern; it was not in any case to make statements about the life that went on around him, or to set forth his opinions about the world. That was only the business of academic painters who were incapable of anything loftier. But in the last few years this attitude has begun to change. Artists are beginning to find that the atmosphere of the ivory tower in which they voluntarily shut themselves up was becoming too rarefied, and that life carried on at that pure level was only possible when events in the external world did not force themselves on the attention too emphatically. As the crisis in the capitalist world grew more and more acute, they found themselves driven out of their seclusion and compelled once more to pay attention to the real world which, though far less pleasant than the dream sphere in which they had previously existed, could no longer be ignored.

We have seen this taking place in England, but, as is nearly always the case in questions connected with the arts, the issue has been much clearer in France, and there the problem has been made the subject of a series of discussions in which some of the most important artists of to-day have taken part. The two principal debates were organised last summer by the Maison de la Culture in Paris, and the results have been published in *La Querelle du Réalisme* (Editions Sociales Internationales).

From the opinions expressed by the various disputants two main problems seem to emerge. The first is: Is the real revolutionary art of to-day to be realistic or non-realistic? The second is: If it is to be realistic, what will this new realism be like?

Our answer to the first question must necessarily depend on what we mean by revolutionary art. At all periods of social disturbance there is always an art which is revolutionary in the sense that it helps to destroy the existing standards, but does not help to build up any new culture. Before the French Revolution of 1789 there was a large section of the aristocracy which was sensitive enough to be disgusted with the existing situation and ready to attack and satirise it, but which did so from within the old system and from the point of view of the old system, without being able to offer anything positive in its place. In a sense, this was a revolutionary art, but only in a strictly negative way. At the same time, a more positive art was growing up which was really the expression of the ideas of the new class which was rising to power. This, on the surface, was much less revolutionary; it seemed in many ways a return to a type of classical art which had been forgotten long before, but underneath it was a more solid movement out of which the art of the succeeding period grew.

Something of the same sort is taking place to-day. There are many kinds of painting which, at the level of painting alone, seem to be revolutionary enough, but which have no roots at all in the rising class. Abstract art and, above all, Surrealism belong to this type. They serve their purpose in destroying the old standards of Capitalist culture, but they have no roots at all in the proletariat, and therefore their contribution cannot lead up to the new culture which will come with the Socialist state.

If we mean by revolutionary art the art which most closely represents the ideas of the rising class, there can be no doubt that the true revolutionary art of to-day will be realistic. The more abstract forms of painting have up till now not gained the approval of the proletariat, which did not produce them, and which cannot find in them what it demands – namely, the expression of its own aspirations and ideas in a form which is easily and widely accessible. Even the supporters of these forms of art do not maintain that their works have been widely welcomed, but they maintain that in time they will be so welcomed. That is to say, their idea of the new culture is that it is to be imposed from above on the mass of the people by an intellectual élite which has evolved this particular kind of art in its own ivory castle. It may well be that when the classless state has been established and all forms of bourgeois art can be regarded from a strictly historical point of view,

these products will fall into their place and be studied, but at
the moment they cannot have an importance for the revolutionary movement.

Popular art has not always been realistic. Fairy-stories and
many forms of primitive art make that quite clear. And
throughout the Middle Ages popular aspirations were forced to
express themselves through a modification of the existing
scheme of thought, that of Catholicism. But since the nineteenth century, when the proletariat began to be an organised
force which was capable of producing its own method of expression, it has been able to do without the various mytholo-
gies which at an earlier stage had been the only available
vehicles for conveying popular ideas. The line of Daumier,
Courbet, the early van Gogh, Meunier, and Dalou is that of the
real art of the growing proletariat, while that of the bourgeoisie
continues towards the abstraction of the twentieth century.

It is of the greatest importance that painters in France at
the present time are beginning to come back to this line. Not
that they are likely to imitate at all exactly the artists of the
nineteenth century mentioned above. The arts have gone so far
as to make a complete return to them impossible as well as
undesirable. Painting cannot go through movements like
Cubism and Surrealism without being in some way permanently changed by them. So that the problem remains: What
will the new realism look like when it finally emerges from the
present chaos? The Cubists have unquestionably made a series
of important discoveries about methods of presenting a subject,
in the way of new compositional devices and new approaches
to formal questions. The Surrealists have investigated new
depths of the subconscious, and thereby added material to the
field of painting which must be absorbed and utilised by it –
provided always that the painter continues to keep his eye
fixed first of all on the outside world.

Certain artists such as Péri have already shown in what way
their training in abstract art can be of use to them in realism,
and there is a passage in the contribution of Edouard Goerg to
the Paris discussion which throws some light on this point,
and also shows the kind of way in which the realistic painter
turns to social use the material which his subconscious throws
up for him. He describes how the painter may be haunted by
certain associations of forms irrespective of any particular content: 'This first scheme is only linear. Then round this linear
structure a certain number of geometrical volumes will group

themselves. For the abstract painter this second stage is final, whereas for the imaginative artist it is only a preliminary.' He goes on to explain how these geometrical forms will suggest certain objects, and in this way the artist will find himself manipulating a group, not of shapes, but of things which have a general interest though they were suggested to him by a particular group of shapes. It will then be the business of the painter to develop his composition so that the objects in it reach their maximum coherence and expressive value. This can usually be done without fundamentally altering the formal structure of the design, for very often a small change in the formal disposition will create an important difference in the material significance of the composition. In this way, the formal hint supplied by the subconscious can be utilised to convey some more rationalised and, therefore, more generally accessible idea.

The discussions are full of hints of this kind which are of interest in showing the attitude of the various disputants in matters of detail, but the most important feature of the whole quarrel is that there is a growing number of artists in France who are no longer prepared to regard painting as a kind of game, but believe that it is, in the phrase of Lurçat, 'an aggressive activity'; who regard the painter as, above all, 'a transformer of energy,' who will not be content to let the painter deal only with still-life and so confine himself to statements about a fruit-to-man relation, but demand that he shall deal rather with the central realities of his period; who believe that 'corn, bread, copulation, revolution, water, space are not small, dirty and unworthy ideas, and that painting has no right to be coy in front of such solid problems.'

(III, 3: 169–71)

Georgi Dimitrov to Writers

A Speech before the Soviet Writers' Association

[June 1935]

Comrades, you know that by a bitter irony of fate I was placed beside Van der Lubbe as one of the accused in the Reichstag fire trial. As a proletarian revolutionary, and a Communist, I was keenly conscious from the start that the German proletariat, the international proletariat, would join issue in this trial with the bourgeoisie, the trial would be an episode in the struggle between Communism and Fascism, between the proletarian revolution and counter-revolution. It goes without saying that when a soldier gets to the front his job is to fight. That is the ABC of the business. I had to fight against Fascism, against national-socialism, against the capitalist system and in defence of the cause of the Communist Party and of the Soviet Union. So much was plain.

But from the early days, from the very first of my Leipzig moves, I was impelled to work at the same time towards certain immediate ends. I have to add, without any beating about the bush, that I had no guarantee of achieving them in the conditions that governed the Leipzig trial, with German fascist dictatorship in the position it then held. At the same time I was sure that it was necessary to try to accomplish these aims, employing every possible means.

What, as a proletarian revolutionary, had I to aim at, when I stood before the Leipzig tribunal? Everyone knew that after the burning of the Reichstag a wave of ferocious and unbridled repression of the working class, and above all of the Communist party, was let loose in Germany. Thousands were thrust into concentration camps, thousands were imprisoned. The German proletariat and particularly the Communist party had to reform ranks under the cross-fire of Fascism. During our short spells of exercise in the courtyard of Moabit prison I marked a gradual change in the state of mind of the prisoners.

In April and May our revolutionary workers who had been arrested and thrown into Moabit, walked with bent heads. In great anguish, they would compare notes secretly, and agree that the German working-class movement had been violently set back. Some of them showed signs of cowardice. June, July, August passed. The new prisoners, comrades recently arrested, showed more spirit. The Leipzig trial focused the indignation of millions of German workers against Fascist dictatorship and the barbaric violence which had been used against the masses. It was necessary, in this trial, to give vent to this hatred of the Fascist régime. It was a platform set on high, and here a blow had to be struck against Fascism. I had to show Communists and other workers, some of whom momentarily hesitated and were beginning to think that the Fascist wave which had been unleashed was insurmountable, that the struggle against Fascism was not only necessary, but possible. It was necessary to offer the example of a living man standing up to Fascism. It was necessary to restore courage to the people, to help to reassemble the forces of the proletariat in the midst of the struggle, and to instil ferments of hesitation and bewilderment among the mass of the National Socialists.

The fight at Leipzig lasted, as everyone knows, for three months. All the rottenness of German Fascism was personified in judges, counsel for prosecution and defence, police spies, officials, and political leaders, during the course of the trial.

The accused themselves formed a curious political assembly. There were among them representatives of the different strata, the different currents, categories, etc. There was a representative of the revolutionary party of the working class, the proletarian revolutionary, and a representative of the lumpen-proletariat, this Van der Lubbe, pitiful, tragic figure: but there was also a representative of the petty-bourgeois elements in the working-class and Communist movement, of the vestiges and survivals of Philistinism and of bureaucracy in the working-class revolutionary movement: the classic example of this type was one whom we all know very well, our ... I was going to say 'ex-comrade'... Torgler.

Comrades, you know that Communism came out of that three months struggle victorious. It conquered thanks to the world mobilization of the working-class and to all honest intellectuals. It conquered because there was a united front agreement which, although unofficial and unwritten, lined up the Communist, Social-Democrat and other parties of the working-class, against German Fascism. Victory was assured because a definite opposition to Nazi provocation began to develop among the lowest masses of the National-Socialists, and showed itself clearly in sympathy for the accused Communists. In the course of the last months of the trial, when the truth began to be clear as daylight, the very police and storm troops expressed what sympathy and esteem they had for me. Hitler and his companions had to take account of that state of mind when it showed itself among their own people.

I recall how Goering, all-powerful boss of German Fascism, came to the court with forty or fifty storm-troops behind him and left after I had been turned out crestfallen in the eyes of his own partisans.

At this meeting of Soviet writers I may be permitted to express a certain astonishment that this Leipzig trial, this enormous collection of material, invaluable stock-in-trade of revolutionary practice and thought, has not been studied or utilized... Take the figure of Van der Lubbe, whose example shows so well how the worker can become a tool in the hands of the class enemy. In the light of the bad example of Van der Lubbe it should be possible to educate thousands of young workers and combat the influence of Fascism on youth.

We are going through a changeful period in the working-class movement in all countries. Comrade Smolianski has recounted a number of facts showing the development of the popular front against Fascism in Germany. In this period, there is more than ever need for 'an active list' of militant revolutionaries to reassemble our forces and proceed to a regrouping of the effective strength of the proletariat, effecting certain distinctions in the ranks of Social-Democracy, bringing the great working masses to their senses. These militant workers 'on the active list' must be educated, they must be educated in the course of the practical struggle, in the midst of difficulties that have to be overcome, educated in the light of concrete examples. What book made a particularly strong impression on me when I was young, and influenced me as a militant worker? I can say definitely that it was a book by Chernychevski, called *What is to be done?*[1]

Such strength as I gained in participating in the working-class movement in Bulgaria, such strength and assurance as I was able to show before the Leipzig tribunal, must most certainly be related to the reading of Chernychevski in my youth.

Where, in our literature, are the heroes of the proletarian movement of Germany, Austria, Bulgaria, China and other countries? Where are the examples to be imitated by millions of workers? (And to educate the young you should show also *negative* examples, though they must be living ones, men of flesh and blood like Van der Lubbe.)

Literature plays an enormous rôle in the education of the revolutionary generation. Help us, help the Party of the working-class, help the Communist International, give us verse, novels, stories, as sharp weapons in the fight; help us by your literary production, to mould the young revolutionary leaders.

There was a time when the revolutionary bourgeoisie struggled bitterly on behalf of its class, employing every means including literature. What book poured ridicule on the vestiges of chivalry? Cervantes' *Don Quixote*. In their hands *Don Quixote* was a powerful instrument in the struggle against feudalism, against aristocracy. The revolutionary proletariat knows the need of a Cervantes – even a little Cervantes would do – able to give us a weapon like that! (*Laughter and applause*.) Fascism is the last effort of the bourgeois class to check the course of history. I read a good deal when I can. I must say that I have not always the patience to read our revolutionary literature. I cannot read it and I cannot understand it. I am not a specialist. (*A burst of laughter*.) But, knowing the masses, the workers and their mentality, I say: No, this is not what the workers want. The worker, opening these books, will find there no standard, no examples to imitate. The man who limits himself to repeating 'Long live the revolution,' is no revolutionary writer! To be a revolutionary writer it is essential to contribute to the radicalization of the working masses, to mobilize them against the enemy.

Forgive me if I speak crudely. You know me of old. I call a spade a spade. But I think that now the Association of Soviet Writers has been formed, you Soviet writers have new and favourable conditions, and new possibilities for a large and fruitful activity.

Writers in the Soviet Union live in the most favourable conditions for their literary production. They live in a country where everything is ebullient, here is construction, enthusiasm, free-play, progress. The atmosphere of the Soviet Union, the very air we breathe, is that of creation.

Abroad revolutionary writers are at grips with exceptional difficulties. They suffer poverty, they are thrown into prison or into concentration camps.

We must place literature more resolutely at the service of the proletarian revolution, in the struggle against Fascism, against capitalism for the mobilization and revolutionary education of the masses. Your books must radicalize the millions of unpolitical or Social-Democratic workers, popularize socialist construction and the great achievements of the Soviet Union. Literature must serve the great revolutionary ideal of millions of workers.

Note

1. N. G. Chernychevski (1828–1889), literary critic and philosopher, wrote his only novel *What is to be Done?* (published 1863) while he was in prison in St. Petersburg. This socialist materialist novel achieved great influence. Lenin adopted the title: Marx wrote that it proved that Russia 'is beginning to participate in the general movement of our century.'

(I, 9: 343–6)

A Letter from Moscow [April 1935]
André Van Gyseghem

The theatre season is drawing to a close; in the month of May many of the theatres will pack up their scenery and properties and take themselves off on a tour of the provinces lasting until August; their itinerary will include such places as the Ukraine, Caucasus, Don-Bas, Kazakstan, Siberia; they will play to backward and wondering peasants and to sophisticates on holiday in the Crimea: to the vivid temperamental Georgian and to the quiet, slow northerner of Novosibirsk. And everywhere they go they will meet with eager audiences greedily absorbing the best that Soviet art has to offer.

Or perhaps, like the Vakhtangov theatre, the company will split up into sections, each group going to its own collective farm with which it has entered into an agreement to lead the cultural life of its workers, and will discuss with them the social implications of their art, of its relations to socialist life, and will embody their discussions in the active production of plays. In this way both the farmer and the visiting artists profit by the contact; the young regisseur in charge of the section is able to enrich his experience by expressing himself in absolute freedom, to experiment in dramatic form, to put into practice ideas which have been formulating in his mind during his work at the Vakhtangov Theatre. In such a way do the young regisseurs find their artistic feet. At the same time they bring all the fruits of their training, their culture and their theatre experience to the eager farmer-students who, while they have their own theatre all the year round, look to this yearly visit from their comrades from the cities to give them the artistic lead that they need for the progress of their work.

They in their turn contribute to the political training of the visiting actors with discussions which arise out of the interpretation of their rôles and of the play as a whole; so each is both teacher and pupil.

Meanwhile the Moscow season has been a success, with a great deal of good material and two or three productions of outstanding brilliance. You can never catch up with the constant and rapid growth in this theatre. New theatres spring up, old theatres experiment in new theatrical forms within the boundaries of their own particular style, new regisseurs appear and startle the town with an experimental production, a whole glut of new plays are produced by such an event as the recent playwriting competition; and as the social and economic state of the country changes so we see the whole face of Soviet dramaturgy changing. I have paid three visits to the Soviet Union in the last three years, and nothing has struck me so forcibly as the rapid switch-over from the mass play to the drama of individual psychological problems related to socialist realism. Just as in life the urgency of teaching people the necessity and advantages of the collective in a socialist state has passed, and the pressing problem of the moment has become the personal attitude, reaction and development of the individual to his work and environment, so we see it reflected in the work of the contemporary playwrights (in spite of what Mr. St. John Ervine says in the *Observer*).

Kirshon's new play, *The Wonderful Alloy*, which won second prize in the play-writing competition and is now running at the affiliated Moscow Art Theatre and at T.R.A.M. (Theatre of Young Workers), is an excellent example of the growing feeling for comedy in the theatre and of the change in subject matter, from the relation of the old intelligentsia to the new life to concentration on the youth of to-day.

In Kirshon's own words: 'the action is centred in a scientific research institute of the aviation industry. A group of young scientists and designers is working to create a new alloy for aviation construction, an alloy that will be extra strong, light and non-corrosive. The brigade consists of very different people, of different personalities. But as a whole this brigade is a "wonderful alloy," a socialist unit of the socialist state.

'We must be able to see the new relations between people, to sense the atmosphere of socialist education and re-education, to find and stress the new features in the people of our country. That was the task I set myself in writing *The Wonderful Alloy*. I tried to show the new youth, the Soviet youth and the new ideas and habits belonging to it alone.'

The play is written with great humour and understanding and if produced abroad would go far to dispel the firm conviction held by most foreigners that all Soviet plays are either an agitation for violence or composed of algebraical formulas.

The classics are increasing in popularity. The 'Maly Theatre' has a new production of Ostrovsky's *Wolves and Sheep*; *Pickwick* is being played at the Moscow Art Theatre; the enchanting production of *Twelfth Night* continues to draw crowds to the Second Moscow Art Theatre, where there is also a new dramatized version of Dostoyevsky's novel, *The Humble and Insulted*; a composite dramatic version of three books from *La Comedie Humaine* by Balzac is a moderate failure at the Vakhtangov Theatre; the Theatre of Revolution is rehearsing *Romeo and Juliet* and the crowning success is *King Lear* at the State Jewish Theatre. About this I shall have more to say in my next letter, but this will serve to show my English friends the very vast field covered by the latest theatre work and of the simply unquenchable thirst for the classics. This is true not only of theatre, by the way, but of literature in general. Books cannot be printed fast enough. As soon as a new edition is out the news spreads like lightning and in a day the whole lot is swallowed up. And of course the important thing is that they are going out to the villages and collective farms in equal quantities, so we find that those young boys and girls in the distant steppes and Tartar villages whose fathers and mothers did not know which way up to hold a book are reading Pushkin and Dostoyevsky, Chekhov and Mayakovsky. Indeed, the place to watch in Russia now is not Moscow and Leningrad but the peasant areas. There the really amazing work is being done.

The play about which everyone is talking is *Aristocrats* at the Realistic Theatre. The director of the theatre, Nikolai Pavlovitch Okhlopkov, is a former student of Meyerhold and carries the latter's theory of conventionalized theatre to its logical conclusion. The theatre is theatre and not life; the audience themselves create the reality out of what they see by association. To consider the stage as though we were looking into a room through a keyhole is absurd – to cause those in the room to behave as naturally as if we could not see them is only to emphasize the absurdity by its un-naturalness.

Okhlopkov has no proscenium. His stage for this production (it varies for every play) is two symmetrically shaped platforms 3 feet high touching at one corner and placed bang in the middle of the theatre – absolutely bare. On one side wall of the theatre rise three panels painted in a design expressive of the seasons which are changed for each act – spring, summer, winter. The whole of one end wall and half the opposite side wall is covered in a plain coloured curtain; again, a different colour for each act. That is all. Properties are carried on and off as they are needed by a crowd of uniformed assistants who are not actually assistants as we use the term but are an integral part of the performance – they make all their entrances and exits in a series of light, swift movements which approach the dance. They are masked.

On this bare platform Okhlopkov produces an intensely realistic play about the building of the Baltic-White-Sea Canal by a crowd of ex-thieves, wreckers and prostitutes under the leadership of the Communist Party – an extraordinary moving epic theme of concrete socialist construction. And what is so interesting is that the play loses none of its realism under the formal conventional treatment. Okhlopkov uses his band of masked assistants in the traditional Kabuki manner. If a character has to telephone, one of the assistants moves swiftly to his side with the telephone and holds it while it is being used. At the end of the conversation he vanishes. If a short scene is to be played behind the table two of them run swiftly on and kneel, holding between them and in front of the characters a piece of cloth in the formation of a hanging table cloth – and off again. The blizzard at the opening of the play is created with music and the crowd of leaping masked figures throwing showers of white confetti high into the air.

Music is used constantly and in a very concrete way. For example, Sonia, the prostitute, is alone on the stage. At this point of the play she is beginning to feel within her the strange stirring of new work and happiness and comradeship: almost she won't admit it to herself, yet it bubbles up and curves the corners of her lips into a smile they have not known since she was a child: she cries and laughs and tears across the stage, flinging herself down and feeling the earth with her whole body – and up again, motionless, strange and still – then off again. And always, following her on noiseless feet, standing just behind her is the masked figure of an attendant – in his hands a violin on which he plays the most poignant music – the music of spring and the new life. Kostia comes on, her lover and as yet an un-regenerate thief – to him her change of mind is weakness and cowardness, he cannot stand the feeling of being left behind – there is a clash of life and death, of the old and the new. To emphasize this the moment he approaches her he snatches the violin out of the attendant's hand – the music stops. Kostia's motif is dominant. And so on.

Afinogenev, author of *Fear* and *The Strange Fellow*, has also chosen this theme for his new play which will probably be produced by the Moscow Art Theatre: and there is yet another by Gorev. This is a striking instance of the close contact between the theatre and the march of events which exists in the Soviet Union and which results in a living Realistic Theatre. Only when we in England are able to show on our stage such projections of contemporary life will our theatre attain true significance.

(I, 7: 269–73)

III. Cultural Critique

This section is distinguished more by emphasis than difference in subject matter from the theoretical section that precedes it. Instead of a discussion of how literature and art function in society generally, the pieces here are primarily concerned with specific cultural situations. Their sense of culture is strongly dialectical – literary and artistic culture shapes people's activity and is shaped by social organisation. Social context is not merely static background; it is a web of active determinants. Whereas the focus in the next section is on the particular context in which specific works are produced, here it is on the larger context. Three of the pieces deal with contemporary society; the fourth deals with the Paris Commune.

Winifred Holtby begins with the material conditions of publishing – numbers of books, social conditions in which reading takes place, commercial considerations, etc. and considers the ideological effect of the culture of the day. The piece is more descriptive than critical and the lack of overt political line evoked some negative response. Literature, even that read as a pastime, is an important transmitter of values. Literary and social values can be improved, Holtby believes, but 'To change literary values involves to a large extent revolutionizing a mode of life'; to change taste we must change social and economic conditions, not just improve library services.

Frank Jellinek deals with the cultural industry from another perspective – the role of artists and writers in the first 'proletarian dictatorship'. In the Paris Commune it was no longer possible to make a meaningful separation of culture and politics. Jellinek extends the perspective produced by the brief experience of the Commune to explain establishment and official cultural responses to painters like Courbet and to draw a lesson for the present: the alliance of intellectuals and workers of the Commune 'proved the necessity, so long as the present society exists, of combining theoretic knowledge and revolutionary action'.

Edgell Rickword deals with the effect of fascism on culture and the spread of attitudes in Britain that point toward fascism. He does not argue in the abstract logic of the class-warfare position, that in effect bourgeois democratic parties are fascist in their collaboration with capitalism, but considers what fascism actually means in the lives of writers who live under it. He also explores the appeal that turned masses of ordinary people toward fascism. Condemnation of fascism is necessary in Britain but it is not politically sufficient; what makes fascism attractive – at the level of ordinary people – must be understood. Rickword examines how the fascist myths of community, sacrifice, service, etc. have a strong drawing power under particular conditions, and he finds the echo in British culture of elements receptive to fascism.

Douglas Garman deals with some of the same conditions discussed by Rickword but without discussing fascist politics. In examining the work of T. S. Eliot he finds an overlap of Eliot's authoritarianism and mysticism and the fascist myth. Garman works close to the texts and his critical practice displays an elaborated sense of the dialectical functioning of culture. Style, for example, is distinct as an aspect of literature but it is not independent; even as style it partakes in the thinking of the time. Eliot is responding to the disintegration of capitalist society and makes his own personal 'idiosyncratic' accommodation in style as well as content. Garman judges that Eliot's work is falling into the same mythic pattern as fascism; it is not useful to call Eliot a fascist but it is helpful for both literary interpretation and political activity to understand the similarities of Eliot's response and fascism.

Garman's approach, even in a political context, remains analytic in character – i.e. he makes his critique in order to provide an understanding which is necessary for action rather than pointing a direction for action itself. On the other hand, Rickword, however subtle his critique and profound his interpretation, always conveys the feeling that his analysis is leading to a political goal – that 'the point, however, is to change it'.

What We Read and Why We Read It

[January 1935]

Winifred Holtby

The invention of the printing press has been acclaimed as one of the greatest achievements of civilized mankind, but recently a tendency has manifested itself to criticize this conclusion. Taste, we are frequently told, is not improving but deteriorating. 'There is some evidence, uncertain and slight, no doubt, that such things as "best sellers" (compare *Tarzan* with *She*), magazine verse, mantelpiece pottery, County Council buildings, War Memorials ... are decreasing in merit,' writes Mr. I. A. Richards of Cambridge in his *Principles of Criticism*. The degeneration of the popular press following Lord Northcliffe's attempt to 'give the public what it wants' has set up an indignant if cynical reaction. In the multiplication of works is little wisdom. Especially, we are told, in the English-speaking countries. The books certainly increase and multiply.

In the first nine months of 1933, four thousand new novels were published, and ten thousand volumes altogether, including general literature and books of reference. A reader, calculated Roger Pippett of the *Daily Herald*, finishing a book every forty minutes and never stopping for meals or sleep, could just about keep up to date with publishers and booksellers. But then he would be obliged to ignore periodicals of every kind, magazines, reviews, trade papers, picture papers, Sunday papers, to say nothing of the whole British Museum Reading Room full of works previously published.

And the ten thousand books are sold. A generous publisher with artistic sensibility and some pride in his own literary reputation may sometimes subsidize an unremunerative author in whose future he believes and whose name upon his list will, he considers, compensate him by adequate prestige for financial loss. But publishers as a rule are not philanthropists; they are business men, out to make a profit from the sale of paper on which are printed words which the public will, in some form or other, pay to read.

The public does read. Every child not medically or physically pronounced incapable by Board of Education officers must be taught how to recognize printed words and how to fashion them himself on paper. Moreover, facilities for reading have increased enormously. It is not merely that books are now easier to obtain than they have previously been – that libraries, private and municipal, have spread to every town and to most villages in the country, that cheap editions, magazines and papers flourish; it is also because the improvement of artificial lighting in the home prolongs the hours in which reading can be comfortably performed; that travel by well-lit public vehicles has become a daily item in the routine of millions of workers, owing to the habit of building residential areas some distance from industrial sites and linking the two by trams and trains and buses; the monotony of these repeated journeys can be forgotten under the spell of changeful print. Shorter hours of work, to say nothing of widespread unemployment, have extended leisure. We can read; we have light, leisure and inclination in which to read; we do read.

But what do we read? That is the question disturbing those interested in standards of public taste. Generalizing roughly and by purely materialistic qualifications, we divide our literature into three classes, books, magazines and papers (Sunday and daily). By far the largest category of books annually published and by far the most widely read, is that of fiction. Novels may again be divided into three types; first the very small, eclectic class of those which have been designed as works of art, which succeed in giving to their readers an aesthetic experience, which commend themselves, on the whole, to a fastidious minority; secondly the large and ever increasing body of competent works of fiction, sometimes hopefully though not always successfully designed by their authors as candidates for the first class, more often intended simply as superior examples of the third; and thirdly, there is the immensely numerous, popular and influential bulk of cheap commercial fiction, produced and marketed for precisely the same reasons that mattresses and boots and bicycles are produced and marketed.

Books of the first category are sold, in so far as they are

sold at all, largely to private purchasers. Readers of *To the Lighthouse, Tobit Transplanted, Memoirs of a Midget, The Corn King and the Spring Queen* or *The Lost Girl* enjoy sufficiently the aesthetic experiences provided by these novels to possess them in order to re-read and discuss them. They enter into their owners' homes as valued and permanent possessions. The second class, published as a rule in their first editions at prices varying between 6s. and 10s. 6d., provide the main material of the circulating libraries. Their range of sale is wide. H. G. Wells and Sydney Horler, Phyllis Bentley and Ethel Mannin, Michael Arlen and Ruby M. Ayres, may flourish as 'Best Lenders,' while their less successful rivals barely contrive to cover their publishers' £20 advance on royalties. It is upon this category that the great intermediate class of the 'novel reading public' browses – those individuals who make out a book list from the reviews and advertisements of the *Sunday Times* and *Observer* (often incidentally failing to recognize the distinction between a review and an advertisement), and who present the list once or twice a week to the assistants at Boots, Mudie's, W. H. Smith's or the Times Book Club libraries. These also are the books provided in response to even vaguer requests for 'a good thriller,' 'a nice love story with no sex in it,' 'something funny' or 'a good solid bit of reading that will last me over the week end.' They are less often bought for permanent possession except in cheap editions or for Christmas presents. They are birds of passage, out of sight out of mind. Their influence is ephemeral, though they have an influence. On their social and ethical values are constructed the social and ethical values of the great middle-classes.

But there is a third and often neglected class of fiction again more frequently bought than borrowed. Here are the formidable ranks of paper-backed novelettes, *The Woman's World Fourpenny Library, Pearson's Sixpenny Novels, The Readers Library*, The *Violet Stories* of Love and Romance at sevenpence, the twopenny, threepenny and fourpenny stories of *Peg's Paper, Poppy's Paper, Betty's Paper, Smart Novels, Week-end Novels, True Love Stories* and *White Heather Novels*. They include school stories and thrillers for adolescents; wild west and detective tales for male readers; for women, romances which bear such titles as *Only a Mill Girl, Was she a Bride?, The Half-day Honeymoon, Unworthy of Her Love* and *A Kiss for Lips that Lied*. These are the books which cover the counters of provincial stationers and suburban tobacconists and newsagents; they are offered at station bookstalls; they are thumbed in trams and propped against sugar basins in cheap cafés; they are read in crowded living-rooms on Sunday evenings; they are smuggled into offices and cloakrooms. They contain the raw material of human drama, unchanged by the transmutations of art, uncriticized by intellectual reflection. They provide in fictitious form those stories of passion, deceit, distress and sudden reversals of fortune, served weekly as fact in *The News of the World*. They are such stuff as dreams are made on, and their little life is rounded on a sleep of the intelligence. Yet though they have nothing to do with art, they satisfy certain appetites which art also sometimes considers. They meet a social need. They have an ethical and even economic influence. They are not without cultural significance, even if that significance is not specially creditable. Together with the cinema, the popular press and the radio, they must be accepted as the common basis upon which the popular imagination feeds.

Detached intelligence is a product of civilization. People living in a state of ignorance, insecurity and limitation of mental interest are cultural egotists. Their first question is: 'What will happen to Me?' Hence the attraction of horoscopes, fortune telling, Old Moore's Almanack, Advice on Personal Problems, Dream books and the more intimate advertisements of patent medicines and beauty treatments. These forms of letterpress appeal immediately to the optimism, the vanity and personal curiosity of their readers. They satisfy that ineradicable desire for a Good Time Coming which lives in the hearts of those whose Bad Time is caused by material circumstances rather than by individual temperament. They partake to some extent of the quality of lotteries, gambling and sweepstakes. Their interest is purely speculative and individual. Advice on etiquette, advice on comeliness, advice on health, advice on love – these are the desiderata sought by readers and supplied by compilers of innumerable pages in the cheaper periodicals.

The wish-fulfilment stories of cheap fiction are closely related to this direct communication of advice. Here the lowest common denominator of individual satisfaction is usually taken to be sexual fulfilment, and *Lady Chatterley's Lover* joins hands with *The Sheik* and *Harem Love*. But running a close second is snob-fulfilment, and Brett Young's *This Little World* and Kipling's *An Habitation Enforced* here point the way to the hundreds of stories founded upon the Cinderella, King Cophetua and the Beggar Maid, or Ugly Duckling themes –

Only a Mill Girl, Maid in her Mother's House, and *The Questioned Coronet.* Jealousy themes, with a direct incentive to self-pity, such as *No Wife to Her Husband* and *A Rival in Her Own House,* provide solace for the lonely, the neglected, the dissatisfied. These forms of entertainment are as direct in their impact upon the ill-nourished imagination as 'Baron Corvo's' *Hadrian VII* has been upon the more sophisticated appetites. They constitute a form of emotional indulgence; but it is a form common to varying standards of intelligence.

There is also the rather more oblique satisfaction to be obtained by escape fiction which opens the gate into another and completely different existence. The popularity of Wild West, Foreign Legion and Gangster fiction among clerks employed in sedentary and monotonous occupations is obvious, just as 'society' novels about guardsmen and peeresses, first popularized by Ouida, provide vicarious experience of luxury to housewives and shop assistants. The sumptuous settings of film scenarios, and the marble pillars of Lyons' corner houses both flatter the same desire.

The particular type of melancholy based upon a sense of the futility of all experience, suffered by sophisticated individuals who already enjoy comparatively comfortable circumstances, plays little part in the lives of people whose poverty, necessity and discomfort have persuaded them that if only these troubles could be remedied, all would be well. The psychological disturbances which assault the imaginations of the authors of *Point Counterpoint* or *The Waste Land* would appear to the readers of *Cheated of Her Child* or *The Son She Sent to Prison* as self-manufactured and superfluous. The simplicity of a mind which accepts physical passion, wealth and social prestige as the enduring goods of life may appear puerile to the more subtle sensibilities of T. S. Eliot's or Aldous Huxley's public. Nevertheless, the distinction between the two types of reader is economic rather than intellectual. Until love, vanity and hunger have been satisfied, the hesitations of Hamlet, the futilities of Mr. Prufrock may appear unimportant. There are sound psychological reasons why Shoreditch should read *Love – the Trespasser,* Ealing *Sorrell and Son,* and Bloomsbury *To the Lighthouse.* There are equally valid reasons why the modestly comfortable suburban housewife wishes to be upheld in her imagination and beliefs, provided with pleasant entertainment and disturbed as little as possible; therefore she clings to the genial optimism of *The Good Companions,* the remote and therefore undisturbing romanticism of *Vanessa* or *Anthony Adverse*, with occasional fluttering excursions into the more exotic atmosphere of *The Green Hat*.

What we read is closely associated with what we are and how we live. To change literary values involves to a large extent revolutionizing a mode of life. There are devourers of puerility in the Blue Train, and Shakespeare makes his most permanent appeal to Old Vic audiences; to every rule are exceptions. Yet it is not quite untrue to say that the springs of taste are social and economic as well as cultural and individual. It is not only by extending library conveniences, reducing the price of classics and discouraging the output of the *Peg's Paper* type of fiction, that we shall raise the standard of literary judgment in this country.

(I, 4: 111–14)

Writers and Artists in the Commune

[December 1934]

Frank Jellinek

In modern revolution there is always a section of the ruling class which splits off to ally itself with the enemies of that class, into which it has been denied entry or with which it has not been able to assimilate itself. The degree of this split will always depend very largely upon local and individual conditions, since this section has no general characteristic of its own. Hovering between two adversaries with strongly defined and contrasting interests, these declassed intellectuals wear a confused and confusing uniform. Courbet[1] made a most revealing sketch for a paper Baudelaire ran during the Revolution of February 1848: upon a barricade stands heroically a figure wearing a workman's blouse above the bourgeois black trousers; he is embellished with a rather battered top-hat. It was typical of Baudelaire in '48; less typical of Courbet himself in 1871.

The history of the lives and work of the younger writers under the Second Empire is simply the history of the police and the censorship. Diabolically, the censorship worked both ways: it prevented the production of works of originality by mobilising 'right-minded opinion' against them; and, as a further result of this, it drove the younger rebels to semi-legal political work *exclusively*, or else to that 'ivory tower' of escape-dreaming and umbilical contemplation, from which only rare and neglected geniuses such as Rimbaud emerged, for twenty years after the fall of the Empire and the Commune.

Until 1868, all political activity could be carried on only in conditions of illegality or semi-legality; therefore the open struggle was waged almost exclusively by the artists and 'pure' writers. Engels has remarked that the political line in nineteenth-century France follows the economic more closely

99

and more immediately than elsewhere. But, with the suppression of politics (Engels was referring only to the period up to 1851), the ideological, superstructural line is even more sensitive, simply because it alone had a field for manoeuvre less directly controllable by the censorship. Hence the extraordinary *political* complexion of such artistic scandals as the Courbet exhibition, the Salon des Réfusés, the prosecutions for obscenity of Baudelaire and Flaubert.[2] In the politically-repressed society, morality became political conformism, the breach of one clause of the Code Napoléon the subversion of the whole.

The case of the painter Gustave Courbet, later member of the Commune, is typical. Courbet himself was a revolutionary individualist. He was not, perhaps, very acutely aware of what the revolution meant before he met and revered Proudhon; but after Proudhon's death in 1865, an event of which he said that it affected him as Napoleon's Coup d'État had done (he had taken to his bed and vomited for three whole days on end), his ideas developed in the same way as those of many former Proudhonists towards the revolutionary activity which his master had deplored. It is simply the 'sanctifying' policy which Lenin has exposed in the case of Marx that represents Courbet as a drunken, vain old man, a great French painter drawn into a criminal adventure by a sort of lunacy and the influence of bad company. This is of course complete nonsense. It is perfectly true that Courbet sat around the cafés with 'low company,' the future leaders of the Commune, propounding his revolutionary theory of 'wringing the coastguard's neck' (absinthe-drinking): 'The first one knocks you down but the second one picks you up:' but his enemies omitted to notice that he had worked for twelve hours before he went down to the café. It is certain, however, that Courbet himself did not look upon his work as revolutionary except in so far as he was doing something different and of course better than the work of the 'official' painters, Scheffer, Bouguereau, Carolus Duran and Co.[3] The theories which became attached to his work were not originally his invention.

It is rather hard to trace any political development in the actual painting of Courbet. There does not seem to be any such development from the *Burial at Ornans* to the later seascapes. But his work remained sufficiently constant, sufficiently revolutionary by its very existence for it to become the text of dialectically progressive theories, and Barbey d'Aurevilly, a disgruntled royalist reactionary, summed up what may be called the police-decision, after the Commune: 'The style is always the man, everywhere, and the style of Courbet the painter expressed the Communard he became, just as the loftier, the more Roman style of the painter David expressed a prouder crime, regicide!' The police-constable's decision is final: sedition is anything with which he does not agree.

The one writer of genius among the younger generation was Jules Vallès. Vallès has suffered the usual fate of the revolutionary artist. Like Courbet, he was maligned, suppressed and neglected in his lifetime; his centenary in 1932 was celebrated with some pomp by a society which still finds it convenient to make poets ambassadors and generals academicians. In his *Jacques Vingtras* series, a dramatised autobiography, Vallès has described the lot of his generation. Driven to revolt by hunger, by the impossibility of expressing his revolt (not that he had not the talent), picking up a job on the boulevard papers and fired time after time for 'showing the tip of the red flag between the lines,' nearing the people in a realization that it was the social, not merely the republican, revolution that was needed, he was greeted by the workers as a leader who could express their inarticulate demands, elected member of the Commune and fought beside the workers in the great battle round the Panthéon, his red sash of office rolled up in newspaper under his arm 'like a lobster.' In his 'Réfractaires' he had debunked once and for all Murger's Bohemia, that legend of the Forties exploded by the Forty-Eight. In his *Rue à Londres*, written in exile after the Commune, he debunked the picturesque humanitarianism of Dickens. And the Academy of 1932 praised the vividness of his style.

His *Jacques Vingtras* explains why there were so many journalists, so few 'pure' writers in the Commune. Such intellectuals as had retired to ivory towers and locked themselves in, or, more commonly, had been locked in by constable-public-opinion, could not be representatives of the revolutionary working class; such as had refused to retreat thither could produce little but journalism, semi-legal until 1868, legal from then on. The number of journalists, however, and caricaturists, the journalists of painting, who took a leading part in the Commune is remarkable. Like Vallès, they were there because they had been driven or attracted towards the workers and were able to express their demands.

The two really important poets of the time, Verlaine and Rimbaud (they had not yet met), took no great part. It is, indeed, highly doubtful if Rimbaud was even in Paris, in spite of his tall stories after the event. His poems on the Commune, especially 'Paris se repeuple' are more valuable than his presence could have been. Verlaine, an unwilling municipal clerk under the Empire, did serve in the Commune's Press Bureau, taking a malicious pleasure in writing savage comments on the press-cuttings of the effusions of his rivals at Versailles. Both he and Rimbaud however, knew many of the Communards, and met them in London in September 1872 in a pub at No.6 Old Compton Street and at the Café de la Sablonière et Provence in Leicester Square.

Most of the journalists and caricaturists who served the Commune got their positions simply because they had shared a café-table or a prison-cell with the leaders. The police, for instance, was almost entirely staffed by caricaturists, simply because they had known Rigault, 'Delegate to the Ex-Prefecture' (the Commune had officially abolished the Prefecture) at the Café Voltaire.

The Commune did not neglect the interests of the artists. Vaillant, a very capable scholar and friend of Marx, was Delegate for Education, which included the administration of the Fine Arts. A member of the International, he attempted to organize his department as an executive for professional unions. He therefore strongly encouraged Courbet and Pottier, a decorative artist who afterwards wrote the *International*, to found an Artistic Federation. This Federation did nothing to define the relation between art and revolution but confined itself to strictly practical matters. The basis of the Federation, according to an elaborate and admirably drawn-up report by Pottier, was to be the free expansion of art removed from all governmental control or privilege; that is, the abolition of the Empire's policy of censorship and bribery. The Federation would never act as artistic judge: 'it does not replace one school by another school, it is only so to speak the driving-force of a mechanism capable of assuring the liberty of all.' No political tendency was required; but Courbet appealed to all artists to repay their debt to Paris by supporting the revolution. A proposal made to the Commune by Billioray, an exhibitor at the Salon des Réfusés, to set up a propaganda committee was never adopted.

The Federation was a great success. More than 400 artists joined. A committee of forty-seven was elected, among whom the most remarkable were Courbet, Corot, Daumier, Manet, Millet, the sculptor Dalou, the architect Delbrouck, the caricaturist and engraver André Gill and the decorative artist Pottier. Naturally, many of those elected had not been consulted first; but it was not a bad selection from the really important and ideologically revolutionary artists of the time. None of the official 'pompiers' was mentioned. Unfortunately, the Federation had no time to do anything important before the Commune fell.

The Commune naturally had no time in its ten weeks of continuous fighting to produce any art of its own except journalism and caricature. But some of this is quite excellent. Vermesch's *Père Duchêne*, a pastiche of Hébert's paper during the French Revolution, with *'foutres* in place of commas,' as a scandalized English correspondent put it, is really good, popular journalism. Vallès *Cri du Peuple* is full of guts. André Gill's caricatures of the Versaillese eminents are first-rate satire. But the great work of the Communards was done in exile. Lissagaray's *History of the Commune* is a work of magnificent eloquence, the work of a fighter through and through (it was probably Lissagaray who fired the last shot from behind the last barricade on Whit Sunday 1871). Vallès *L'Insurgé*, in the 'Vingtras' trilogy, is a savage and vivid account of the experiences of the revolutionary intellectuals. Vuillaume, Vermersch's fellow-editor, produced an admirable journalistic reconstruction in his *Cahiers Rouge*. Lucien Descaves, collaborating with Hippolyte Varlin, brother of the Eugène Varlin who was one of the Commune's heroes, described the exile (unfortunately not the London group, which is still to be done) in *Philémon*. Pottier's songs were sung by two generations of marching workers.

They have been forgiven or forgotten by the French bourgeoisie which still attempts to enforce a moral and commercial censorship. Courbet has a street named after him in the plutocratic district of Passy. His work for the Commune's Artistic Federation, his extremely sensible speeches in the Commune Council are not mentioned in the official biographies, which spend their space proving that he did not pull down the Vendôme Column, but merely said he would like to see it 'deflated.' But once again the police-decision is final. At his trial, where he was sentenced to six months and the repair of the Column at his own cost, the public prosecutor declared: 'Occupying a relatively high rank in society, enjoying a deserved reputation as a painter and independent means due to his talent, Courbet has associated with the men of disorder in their criminal attempts.' As he was escorted back to his cell, someone asked him what he was going to do now. 'A seascape,' replied Courbet; but his warder told him that he was not in jail to amuse himself.

The Commune was premature. Forced fatally back on the defensive by its own error in not at once attacking, the Commune split: it seemed that the intellectuals were reverting to their own class background, the outworn ideas of 1848 and 1793. But a section of them – and, very significantly, almost all those who were most efficient in their particular work (including Courbet and Vallès) – realized the lesson formulated again and again by Marx and Engels: that a correct revolutionary line and the experience of revolution were of far greater importance to the working-class movement than the local victory or annihilation of one phase in the historical international class-struggle, even though that phase, the setting-up of a proletarian dictatorship for the first time in history, was itself of colossal importance: the Commune would be the great school of the revolutionary working-class movement.

It is this section of the Communards, about equally composed of intellectuals and workers, that provides more than the traditional barricade-alliance: it proved the necessity, so long as the present society exists, of combining theoretic knowledge and revolutionary action: what to do and how to do it: 'the teachings of the classics and propagandists, the ABC of communism, to the ignorant the realization of their position, class-consciousness to the exploited, and to the class-conscious the experience of revolution.' (Brecht: *Die Massnahme.*)

Notes

1. Gustave Courbet (1819–1877), perhaps the first French painter who set himself the task of painting subjects from ordinary life realistically. Under the Commune he was elected to the Chamber and after the counter-revolution he was condemned to pay £12,000 for the destruction of the Vendôme Column. He died in exile.
2. The *Salon des Réfusés*, famous exhibition of rejected masterpieces, was opened in 1862 when the jury of the French *Salon* finally refused to accept the unconventional paintings of Manet and his followers. This was five years after the government had prosecuted Baudelaire successfully and Flaubert unsuccessfully for writing the two key works of nineteenth-century French literature.
3. Scheffer made sentimental religious paintings. Bouguereau painted *Love Disarmed, Love Victorious, Love in a Shower, Prayer*, and so on.

(I, 3: 83–6)

Straws for the Wary: Antecedents to Fascism [October 1934]

Edgell Rickword

The cynical, exasperated or plaintive individualism which marked the most 'advanced' literature immediately before and just after the 1914–18 war, soon began to yield to a search for values, a desire for order, or even for a 'revelation.' So side by side with the literature expressing mal-adjustment between the writer and his social environment (Lawrence, Eliot, Joyce, Huxley, etc.), there grew up a clinical literature attempting to diagnose and prescribe for the pathological condition which, in many cases, the writers recognized in themselves. In his creative work Lawrence tried to depict the 'primitive' sort of life in which he would have been able to function naturally, and Eliot poultices his poetic malaise with dreams of a world of catholic, classic tradition which would restore the human dignity the loss of which he has consistently exploited as the subject matter of his poems. Middleton Murry, a writer with no creative gift, looked for a 'revelation' in the work of creative writers, from Jesus Christ to Lawrence, and though his meanderings are of no intrinsic importance, the fact that he, like the others, has concentrated much of the intellectual discussion of recent years round him, shows that a large number of thinking people are also on the search for a 'final' solution of their problems. The pursuit of pleasure, the enjoyment of wit, the exercise of a sceptical intelligence, all the licensed relaxations of a prosperous economic dictatorship, were found to be 'not enough.' Men wanted 'to get in touch with God again,' as the more naïve of the panacea-mongers phrased it, as usual disguising reality with transcendentalism. What had actually happened was that the licensed amenities mentioned were no longer available even to the small number of the middle-class who had before been allowed access to them. Pleasure, and even

105

wit, had by means of the film and heavily capitalized publishing, irretrievably become *commodities*; and even the pose of 'cultural values,' which had persisted through Matthew Arnold's lifetime, was no longer seriously kept up. (Intelligence, when bought, becomes something else: a compound of ingenuity and sophistry; and much of it is being perverted in the press and publicity ramp to-day, since even the intelligent man must live.) The intellectual had become a slave as much as the wage-earner. Though the cause was not immediately analysable, such people, being by nature sensitive, felt the death in the veins of the society they were condemned to live in, and expressed it in their despair or in their desperate romantic escapes. As it happened, enough of the old economic structure was left to provide some sinecures, a small audience, a little income, to enable some of them somehow to exist without entirely surrendering; but this unreal existence, this not belonging to a living community, either frustrated them or drove them to seek the essential contacts in those modes of thought which are hung about like fly-papers to catch the desperate – the immaterial, the spiritual, the idealistic. Such are the advantages, for the rulers, of literary education.

The conviction of the advance of reason and of the progress of social reform had been severely checked by the forced participation of many of the intelligentsia in the War. Afterwards, many who could not join the indifferent crowd fell for the anti-rationalist revival which naturally flourished in the soil provided by the slaughter of so many generous and humanitarian illusions. Among the more sharply defined reactions may be noted the strong philosophical movement in France, echoed by *The Criterion* in England, which set to work to re-assert the primacy of belief, and by a juggling with paradoxes, to spread the conviction that an act of faith is the highest expression of reason. Vulgarized, of course, from the respectable plane of neo-Thomist syllogistics, but exploiting the same emotional need, is the unquestioning allegiance demanded in all the Fascist expositions and apologetics.

A further stage in the sensitive registration of social decay was marked by the publication of W. H. Auden's *Poems* in 1930. Here was complete realization of the disintegration of the society to which the poet belonged and of the imminent collapse of the whole system. The comparative popularity of these poems was no doubt due, apart from their technical merits, to the fact that they expressed what a younger set of people were feeling as a result of the further stage of decay that society had reached since the writers we first mentioned had formed their sensibilities:

Financier, leaving your little room ...
The game is up for you and for the others,
Who, thinking, pace in slippers on the lawns
Of College Quad or Cathedral Close.

The sense of imminent catastrophe, of snatching a joy in the moment of precipitate collapse, was seductively presented. Also contempt for the old, and for intellectual 'knowing,' are themes which may be heard in less poetic quarters:

Knowledge no need to us whose wrists enjoy the chafing leash,
Can plunder high nests; who sheer off from old like gull from
granite. ...

One does not, of course, ask for a political system from a poet, but there is a disarming, boyish charm about this, and its catching-on is not without political significance, at a time when Fascism is popularized as a 'Youth Movement.'

Such, briefly, is the situation of the bourgeois intellectual to-day. 'Sinking ship psychology' would perhaps sum it up. In such a situation, whatever reactions there are, are likely to be extreme ones, and when the prevailing philosophy is non-rational (even the non-Christian philosophers like Whitehead have a God, called in Whitehead's case, I think, emergent evolution) it is easy to plunge into excess: cynicism or sentimentality, blatant hedonism or foolish idealism, are the alternate sides of the medal that bourgeois culture is dying to offer to its youthful supporters.

In material ways, the economic crisis has very definitely worsened the conditions for the intellectual worker. There are fewer periodicals in which he can place articles, and the tendency to concentrate all a firm's selling power on a few best-sellers makes it almost impossible for him to get more than a pittance from book sales. A certain number with literary facility may be absorbed in the Publicity Agents' copy-writing studio, despising the work; but, in general, the majority of the intellectual youth is unemployed – and un-employable as intellectuals.

There were many young men in Germany for whom a

brown shirt, a barrack-room bunk, and a knuckle-duster, were the only means of keeping alive. But, even more important, at the same time they were provided with easily acceptable emotional stimuli, and the intoxication of a myth. And there, among other categories, the intellectual, quite simply and for his own sake, Aryan ex-soldier though he be, is scheduled as one of the causes of whatever may be allowed to be not quite perfect in the Third Reich.[1]

'Oh but,' say the English intellectuals, 'it won't come to that in this country.' But it is not necessary for government to take the catastrophic Mosley form, for conditions to worsen still more for the intellectual. Subtly, much more subtly than the blustering imitators of the continental dictators could conceive, the literary output of the time can be *gleichgeschaltet*. A critic gradually finds his taste for the 'social problem' novel waning; a publisher observes that a very dull novel about an English village which he only published because he was short of a title in his list, has a most marvellous press and sells steadily. There is no need for fierce prohibitions from the Minister of Culture, for lists of 'approved subjects' from the Minister of Propaganda, in a country so happily governed. Such is the trend to-day, as reflected in recent successes, towards quiet studies of ordinary, unsophisticated people, to books about the countryside; and that 'other opium' of the bourgeoisie, the detective novel, of course flourishes with every assistance from the high seats of culture.

The premium thus put on simplemindedness, is, at present, almost negligible compared to the compulsory infantilism to be expected of the Corporate State. In reviewing the output of fiction recently published in Germany, *The Times Literary Supplement* (July 26) notes: 'certain writers may have disappeared from the publishers' lists, while certain other writers or kinds of writing, may have achieved a prominence they never enjoyed in the days of German parliamentary democracy' – a sentence which veils the brutal realities of exile or murder, and the subsidized mediocrity of the *National-Socialist Writers' Society* monopoly with typical *Times'* gentility. And wanting to show that bourgeois intellectual independence is not entirely subdued, the best it can say is: 'But there is still a remainder, and a not unimportant remainder, whose expression is not influenced, or if influenced at least not distorted, by the triumph of National

Socialism.' The *Observer* reviewing Euringer's *German Passion*, 1933, remarks that it might pass unnoticed but for the fact that it has received special recognition from the Propaganda Minister as 'the best play of the year'; and goes on to say that it is 'hardly valuable as literature.' It is interesting to notice that in this production the usual categories of those who 'betrayed' the soldiers at the Front are extended to include the intellectuals, and now comprise 'the phantasts, littérateurs, criminals, democrats, Jews, and Marxists.'

Since the economics of fascism inevitably leads to want, the ideology of its literature is full of eulogies of the beauties of sacrifice (in a world overstocked with everything) and the superiority of spiritual to material enjoyment. 'None of you is without a 'ome,' the 'serio-comic' workman exhorted us in Eliot's *The Rock*, 'but God 'as no 'ome. Build 'im one.' And this was at Sadler's Wells, within two minutes' walk of some of the most abominable slums.

Psychologists have observed that where any repression is at work, the individual instinctively reverts to earlier forms of satisfaction, e.g. a desire to be mothered by a woman instead of loving her. The emotional foundations of Fascism, and hence its art phantasies, are predominantly adolescent. Dressing-up, the gang-spirit, the devotion to the Leader, were an important part of existence up till the age of fourteen. And what are Hitler, Mosley or Mussolini like, more than those big backward boys who in every school get stuck in the Fourth Form, and who by a mixture of bullying and toadying attract a certain amount of unattached idealism to themselves?

This theme of the Leader is well brought out in an article in *The Vanguard* (July 1934) called *Fascism as I see it*, which provides a very well-developed case of leaderolatry. It is written by the Hon. Nancy Mitford, an ingenuous lady who admits that it is hard to answer people when they ask her 'what exactly is Fascism?' and complains: 'They have before them the examples of Italy and Germany to show how the Fascist idea has operated in those countries. What more do they want to know?' Nothing, one would think. But she goes on to tell us about 'the great and good Leader' that Fascists need, and who, 'we British Fascists' believe, has at last arisen, and 'that our Leader, Sir Oswald Mosley, has the character, the brains, the courage and the determination to lift this country from the slough of despond in which it has for too long weltered, etc., etc.' In the elegant society beauty of the portrait which accompanies this instructive article, we ought to recognize as well a heroine of outlook rare in these degenerate days, not shrinking from the contemplation of death or indelicacy in her ambition to get level with those great examples, Fascist Italy and Germany. For how is the great and good Leader to deal with the doddering politicians whose highest hope is 'that from day to day they may continue to creep about the halls of Westminster like withered tortoises?' The answer is contained in a sentence so outstanding that it deserves wider publicity than it can have achieved in the schoolroom periodical it appeared in:

'No wonder they (that is the Cabinet Ministers) dread that day when the real sun shall dawn with a heat that will shrivel all those who are not true at heart, that day when the Leader shall stand by their dissolute bedsides, a cup of castor oil in the one hand, a goblet of hemlock in the other, and command them to choose between ignominy and a Roman death.'

No Fascist leader attempts to gain intellectual respect; it would not be worth while. They make no claim to efficiency, or understanding, and depend entirely on the mysterious principle of *Führerschaft* – Leadership. Hitler, after having shot the greater number of his lieutenants, demands 'Blind obedience.' 'Hitler's Will is Justice,' Goering bluffs. And for a time many well-intentioned people are taken in. And it is when no discussion of principles, when only emotionalism and intuitionism are encouraged, as to-day, that the danger of falling for some such charlatan is most acute. Herbert Read, in a poem called 'The Nuncio' (*Life and Letters*, March 1934) has a Leader, or rather a Leader's mate, who, in spite of his precept 'evading force by the use of mental agility' says much as to the organization of society that would commend itself to a philosophic Fascist. Read describes first of all the expectant crowd of elect disciples, then after a fanfare and a sudden cry of heralds, the ceremonial entry of the Nuncio, quite in the style of Mosley's Olympia Circus. The Nuncio's message is too long to detail here, but we may doubt whether all the hush and reverence was worth while when we hear that the centre of this hieratic system is 'an inner redoubt under lock and key' containing 'the lost lineaments of goodness, truth and beauty.'

Here, as in Nancy Mitford, we may note the emotional, school-girlish attitude to the Leader. Having heard the beans spilled:

> we who had listened
> suspended in stillness
> surged like a sudden tide
> towards the dais where he stood.
> But Starr
> checked our rash
> onward rush
> held us with uplifted hand
> and to us gave this last command. ...

Mosley quotes with sympathy the saying of a great man of action: 'No man goes very far who knows exactly where he is going.' Read's Nuncio was quite in type in being so vague, and the deficiency can, of course, only be made up by arousing this emotional, disciple relationship to cover the day to day gambles of the Fascist 'attitude of mind.'

After the 'mystery of leadership' comes the 'mystery of patriotism.' The English are apt to sneer superiorly at the German professors and their readiness to teutonize everything, even the Virgin Mary, at the dictates of State policy. But a lot of extraordinarily chauvinistic theories were propounded by the British Universities during the War, though most of them were discreetly dropped afterwards. The beginnings of a philosophy of race hatred are provided by Sir Arthur Keith's *The Place of Prejudice in Modern Civilization*,[2] and it is significant that this is quoted with approval in a eulogistic review by Douglas Jerrold of Yeats-Brown's *Dogs of War*.

The weakening of the intellectual opposition to war mentality has become most noticeable in the last few months. Minds are being prepared not merely to think that war is not so bad, but even to applaud when it is being as blatantly glorified as it ever was by a Prussian philosopher like Treitzche, who was so soundly abused in 1914. *Dogs of War*, which even a year ago would have been coldly received, was seriously and even enthusiastically reviewed in July 1934. Some few reviewers, did, fortunately, treat it with the contempt it deserved. But Clifford Sharp, for example, an ex-editor of the *New Statesman*, was so amazed at its intellectual power that he could not find any arguments against the superiority of the attractions of war compared with those of peace.

Yeats-Brown is a member of the January Club, the Fascist highest 'social' organization, which includes as its chief intellectual ornament Sir John Squire, an ex-Fabian, recently rewarded with a knighthood for his long services in keeping any taint of serious living interest out of the very extensive literary domains which have come under his sway.

Aldous Huxley, who from his novels one would judge to have passed his life without much contact with the variety of human beings (he has moved widely about the surface of the earth, it is true, but, as he himself notes, partnered with an *Encyclopædia Britannica* and a typewriter, whose demands allow but little time for thought) yet feels competent to pronounce on the cause of wars. This is an example of the helpless type of intellect which, though it may detest war, yet thinks of it as 'inherent in human nature,' and in many cases gets an emotional kick out of this looking down on the mass of slaughtering humans from its own icy heights of dispassionate understanding. Ruminating on the present Anglo-American struggle in the Chaco, Huxley decides that war is a periodic orgiastic outburst, occurring spontaneously (see *Beyond the Mexique Bay*). This is surely unsubstantiated by history and common experience; certainly it is no less disastrous than the militaristic position.

Fascism, which makes direct for war, as the Fascists themselves make no attempt to deny, cannot afford to allow any intellectual liberty. National or Coalition Governments are bound to make war in the end, and in a state of war, what little liberty the intellectual has now will inevitably be taken from him. There must not be any hesitation in resisting these two things, not only in their more obvious physical manifestations, but in the subtler emotional forms they take in literature, philosophy and art.

Notes

1. 'Erich Bloch is another in this category who has been beaten and tortured in spite of his record as a flying officer in the war. ...
    Unless they leave Germany on being released from concentration camps, authors and writers are by no means at the end of their struggles. Publishers and editors refuse to take their stories and articles.' (Alan M. Wells, *Bookman*, August 1934).

A writer in *The Blackshirt* (August 3rd, 1934) discovers an antagonism between culture and agriculture and advocates, or rather threatens, all hands to the plough. Under Fascism, no doubt, Editors would be compelled to publish his nonsense. Imprisonment in a German concentration camp has the same intention behind it, to quell that mental activity which is so frequently stigmatized in Nazi theory as inimical to Germanic culture.

2. This little work, remarkable for its fallacious logic even more than for its antiquated anthropology, is in the form of a Rectorial Address, which Sir Arthur thought a suitable argument to instil into the hundreds of young students of Aberdeen University who had elected him their rector (1931).

(I, 1: 19–22, 24–5)

What? ... The Devil? [October 1934]
Douglas Garman

In a recent work of literary criticism, Eliot explicitly declared
his preference for 'an audience which could neither read nor
write,' and though he was then speaking of poetry, one felt
that he was by way of claiming a greater licence than may
safely be allowed even to a poet. Here,[1] where as he says he
'ascended the platform ... only as a moralist,' he appears frequently to be speaking from the further, implicit, assumption,
that his audience will not think. Again and again he begs a
crucial question, either by referring it to an unspecified arbiter,
or by an appeal to a kind of knowledge his hearers cannot be
expected to have experienced. This is the method of the ardent
convert rather than of the serious expositor of a point of view,
and it is no defence of it to disclaim, as he does, 'any intention of arguing or reasoning,· or engaging in controversy with
those whose views are radically opposed to' his. Since it is his
wish to preach 'primarily to those who ... are possibly convert-
ible,' it is but a poor reflection, either on the quality of his
creed or upon the intelligence of his desired converts, that he
hopes to dispense with argument – unless, of course, he claims
divine inspiration.

We need not concern ourselves, however, with his intentions.
What particularly makes his position interesting is that, before it
had become a fashionable truism, he had realized the ineffective-
ness of the prevalent attitude of romantic, *laissez-faire* liberalism.
In this he was not, nor would he claim to have been, original;
but of the group of writers who gathered round T. E. Hulme just
before the war, he has attained the most influential position and
is listened to with most respect. Though his approach was then a
strictly literary one, his essay on *Tradition and the Individual
Talent*, published fifteen years ago in the *Sacred Wood*, carried, as
good literary criticism must, implications and possibilities of application outside the field of mere literature. It was an argument

114

against the excessive indulgence of individualism in Art, and therefore in favour of authority. At that time it took him no further than a necessarily vague formulation of classicism, but the seriousness that distinguished the essay suggested that he would not, as so many of his contemporaries have done, find lasting satisfaction in an aesthetic definition. Unlike Ezra Pound, for instance, who, having locked himself into an ivory tower and self-consciously hidden the key, now petulantly abuses the world at large for not visiting him, he has continued his search for a system of thought which would, by again relating art and society, nourish the former and be of service to the latter. To that extent, the trend of his thought was potentially marxist. But, if the widened scope of his later criticism was not unexpected, it has proved at least equally disappointing, not only in the conclusions it has led to, but also in the very marked falling off in the vigour and quality of their expression; for as a prose-writer pure and simple, Eliot has declined. The surface of his prose remains much the same, but where it was once solidly supported it now rings hollow: the virile prudence which was characteristic of the *Sacred Wood* has devolved into a method of avowal and retraction which is frequently completely negative; the earlier scrupulousness of definition has given place to dogmatism; and where once he could crystallize his dislikes in an impudent, but pertinent and amusing understatement – for instance, his remarks on Milton and Goethe – he is now inclined simply to sneer. These are matters of style, but they are to be accounted for by the ideas that lie behind; and to these *After Strange Gods* is a handy index.

Briefly, and I think fairly, the gist of these three essays may be taken to be a reaffirmation of the importance of tradition in life and literature and an attempt to modify and make more precise the meaning of tradition by associating it with the concept of christian orthodoxy. In the second he goes on to illustrate from the work of certain contemporary writers[2] 'the crippling effect upon men of letters, of not having been born and brought up in the environment of a living and central tradition,' and lastly he discusses the 'far more alarming consequences ... resulting from exposure to the diabolic influence.' It is here he concludes that 'tradition by itself is not enough; it must be perpetually criticized and brought up to date under the supervision of what I call orthodoxy.' Clearly, then, it is of the first importance to ascertain what he does call orthodoxy and what he means by tradition.

There has always been a suspect morbidity about Eliot's

preoccupation with tradition, even when his preoccupation was
enabling him to render a very real service to criticism. It is as
though he were always nervously conscious of approaching it
from the outside, so that he has often been guilty of the twin
vices of the *parvenu*: assumed humility and dogmatic supercili-
ousness. Here, more than ever, he has the air of a Board of
Agriculture expert sent to lecture to the ignorant practical
farmer; conveniently forgetting, what he knows very well when
he writes of Gerard Manley Hopkins, that 'to be converted ...
is not going to do for a man, as a writer, what his ancestry
and country for some generations have failed to do.' It is all
very fine for him to assert that what he means by tradition
'involves all those habitual actions, habits and customs ...
which represent the blood kinship of "the same people living
in the same place,"' but his suspicious record of vagrancy
detracts from the force of his opinion: it is like Hitler, the
Austrian, proclaiming the virtue of nordic ancestry. Nor are his
strictures on Irving Babbitt any the more convincing for being
uttered by a fellow American. 'The very width of his culture,
his intelligent eclecticism, are themselves symptoms of a narrowness of tradition, in their extreme reaction against that
narrowness,' is a judgment that recoils; and though he may
disparage Babbitt's 'addiction to the philosophy of Confucius,'
he admits to having himself spent two years of his life dram-
drinking at the fountain of Pantanjali. But it is not Eliot's
knowledge of tradition that is in question. He knows what it
means only too well, and it is precisely that which makes it in
his hands such a dangerous critical tool: he is so busy knowing
what it means that he hasn't had time to get the feel of it.
Not, of course, that Eliot is without tradition: but the one into
which he was born – that of New England, and presumably of
Protestant-agnostic New England – is not the one under whose
banner he fights.

Yet though, while accepting the value and necessity of
tradition, one rejects Eliot's interpretation of it,[3] and more particularly his application of it, it is at least clear what the term
means for him. His orthodoxy is a very different pair of shoes.

What one must insist upon is that an orthodoxy as vague as
Eliot's is a futile criterion of literature and morals. How futile
becomes apparent when he applies it patronizingly to discredit
the spiritual explorations of Yeats, or to disparage the 'deplorable religious upbringing' of Lawrence. What, after all, one is
justified in asking, was Eliot's own? The Episcopal Church of

America, or some form of that protestant-agnosticism to the decay of which he traces so many shortcomings? There is little evidence here of a man writing from strong traditional conviction. Rather, it would seem, that the morbid fascination of tradition, commented upon earlier in this review, takes the form, *vis-a-vis* orthodoxy of a disdainful obscurantism. His primer abounds with such phrases as 'the danger of suggesting to *outsiders*' and when reviewing the intrusion of the diabolic into modern literature, he yet fears that his readers 'may still have a very inaccurate notion of what Evil is': but when it comes to more exact definition of the terms he uses, he contents himself with referring us 'to more philosophical writers.'

Such a mixture of zealotry and priggishness, of assurance and pretended humility, would be amusing if it were not that whatever Eliot writes is backed by a considerable reputation. In a world which is hungry for some form of order and authority, there will be many who will grasp at the authority that is here so speciously offered them without much enquiry as to its value; and when they are ultimately forced into political alignment there is no doubt which it will be. It is true Eliot himself, in his devotional drama, *The Rock*, dismisses Redshirts and Blackshirts in the same offhand manner, but the despairing contempt with which he treats them both does not disguise his sympathies. Though he declares through the mouthpiece of the chorus that 'it is better to suspend judgment,' the whole bias of his play proves that he has already made it, just as the whole trend of his later criticism is to the effect that we can no longer afford to suspend it. In this he is a typical case for marxist diagnosis. Confronted by the breakdown of capitalist society, his reaction against liberalism is seen to be merely the relinquishing of an untenable position, and his conversion to religious orthodoxy – his particular choice is a personal idiosyncrasy – is a last attempt to elude the fundamental political issue. The graph of his personal development is closely parallel with that of Fascism: just as the latter, having rejected democracy, strives to perpetuate the capitalist system in a disguised but more stringent form, so Eliot, the bankrupt Liberal, turns to a creed which, while proclaiming its authority, gives full play to his individualist bent. In both cases it is simply calling the same thing by a different name: capitalism becomes the corporate state; tradition, orthodoxy. And as the alternative to the one is Communism, the alternative to the other is dialectical materialism.

Notes

1. *After Strange Gods. A Primer of Modern Heresy.* By T. S. Eliot (Faber & Faber).
2. It is worth noting that though he asserts 'I am sure that those whom I have discussed are among the best,' he has just previously spoken of 'some of the *few* modern writers whose work I know.' One does not cavil at his choice, but the proximity of the two sentences is typical and significant. One is left to infer, either that Eliot, as it were, 'only knows the best people,' or that he relies upon unspecified, but uncontrovertible, authority.
3. To the extent to which tradition is, as Eliot insists it is, a *living* force, the marxist interpretation of history is essentially traditional: while it insists upon the inevitability of revolutions, these breaks in continuity are subsumed within the larger dialectical process. Indeed the tradition expressed in historic materialism reduces all others to merely local and fugitive significance.

(I, 1: 34–6)

IV. Critical Methodology and Specific Studies

This section includes pieces that characterise a Marxist critical approach and specific critiques that make clearer the criteria and how they are supposed to be employed.

In 'Revolutionary Art Criticism' F. D. Klingender begins with 'the problem of the standard for revolutionary art criticism' and attacks Montagu Slater's praise of the Soviet sculptor Dimitri Tsapline. 'Remove the Soviet Star from the helmet of the "Red Soldier"', says Klingender, 'and you are left with a head that might have been taken straight from any one of a whole series of Bismarck towers and similar monuments of Wilhelmian Germany.' Slater, he says, is shirking his 'duty of applying the only Marxian test of relevance to the problems of social reality'; revolutionary art criticism must escape 'the shackles of bourgeois formalism' and help artists to create a revolutionary style. 'Silently assuming that a Soviet artist "can do no wrong" is the worst possible crime.'

Slater said, in a brief response, that he hoped to reply in the next number. It was Ralph Fox, not Slater, who replied, and in unusually vitriolic terms. In 'Abyssinian Methods' he says of 'Colonel Blimp-Klingender' that the best thing 'would be to deprive him of pen and ink for the rest of his life'.

Fox attacks Klingender for the narrowness of his criteria, treating his *general* proposals as if they were specific, and he avoids Klingender's more detailed comments on Tsapline's work. Yet Fox's own criteria partake of an equally vague generality; he demands of Klingender, 'Where in all this conception is dialectic?' This is made more specific when he expands the question to 'where is the idea of inner development, where the connection between form and content?'

Both Klingender and Fox are looking for a Marxist criticism that is multi-dimensional and which understands art and politics in dialectical relation. The apparent differences they discover in positions that are fundamentally so close suggests

119

how early a stage they are at in the development of Marxist critical method.

Edgell Rickword, in his review of Philip Henderson's *Literature*, characteristically pays attention to how readers respond to what is written. For example, it is not of primary importance to him that Henderson is dogmatic but that because of his dogmatism readers will not listen to his argument. For Rickword the schematic thinking that Henderson displays fails to deal adequately with what is actually there in the literature and the society, and the schema employed obscure the conflicts in the literature which in fact indicate the process of change. Rickword's other writing displayed impressive theoretical power; his insistence that abstraction is inadequate, that criticism must look at what happens in literature at the level of actuality for individuals, is not a lesser rigour but a more thoroughgoing Marxism.

In 'The German Drama: Pre-Hitler' Bertolt Brecht explains his conception of theatre and relates the origin of 'Epic Theatre' to the need for theatre to deal with what the audience recognised as the important issues of the day. The piece defines an approach that insists on theatre's relation to the real world and in effect puts forward a set of critical principles.

Bert Lloyd, in his review of Herbert Read's *Surrealism*, accepts the justice of the surrealists' claim that 'polemical art', because it is all exterior, explains nothing. Rhetoric does not make the revolution, as many others in *Left Review* said, and a revolutionary rhetoric does not mean that art will have a revolutionary effect: 'We all know how sad it is to see politically left artists preoccupied with painting academic pictures of muscle-bound workers with a hammer and sickle appearing in the sky above them, or of *Daily Worker* canvassers in action.' Lloyd speaks of the surrealists' treatment of Courbet, who was revolutionary without having a revolutionary subject matter, and says that they mistakenly assume that Picasso's and Max Ernst's similar challenge to formal conventions makes them revolutionary. They are not; 'the underlying message of their work is not conducive to social or revolutionary responsibility' and it is false to present it as such.

Lloyd accepted that the English surrealists had raised considerable support for the Spanish government, even if he found no political virtue in their art; and Herbert Read and Hugh Sykes Davies, in their reply in the next issue, were not unsympathetic: 'Mr. Lloyd repeats the old criticism that Surrealism is irrational and anti-rational, but in such a profitable form that he deserves a reply.' They agree that the surrealists do have a great emphasis on the irrational, but that is because they wish to preserve 'a clear reason'. They are trying to develop 'a socially responsible lyrical tendency', but surrealism is only at the beginning of its development.

'The Detective Story' by Alick West extends over two issues, which allows him space to describe the development of mystery writing and the novel of terror, as well as dealing with its ideological functions. The earlier detective novels created an identification of authors and readers with crime and the criminal, which West relates to 'the confused revolutionary and reactionary feeling of the romantic movement'. In the next stage of development identification is with the detective, whose deductive powers protect against an unruly world. The contemporary detective novel depends on an interrelation between a complex reality and the criminal act; the shift back to appreciation of the ingenuity of the crime has an element of sympathy for disturbance of the social order. West reaches a neat dialectical conclusion that does not overstate any revolutionary claims in its social analysis: 'The detective story is also a sign of revolt against decaying capitalism, while endeavouring to make that revolt harmless.'

Barbara Nixon, in 'Plays about Trade Unionism', offers a critique of Miles Malleson's *Six Men of Dorset* and compares it to what she regards as a more successful play, the American play *Stevedore*. The context of her argument is the political functioning of the plays; whether or not they are successful, she explains, depends not on their political position but on their formal, aesthetic, dramatic development. In making her judgement of *Six Men of Dorset* she articulates clearly and succinctly a relation between dramatic construction and political message: 'The play suffers because it is an over-faithful reproduction of the particular, and makes no attempt to reach the universal.' Although it is historically accurate, it does not represent events in a way that makes it relevant to the present day.

In a short review of Charlie Chaplin's *Modern Times*, Elizabeth Coxhead says that the industrial subject provides a hilarious absurdist humour but she is clear that, because it lacks a coherent perspective, the film cannot serve as a serious critique of industrial capitalism.

Stephen Spender, reviewing *Phoenix*, praises Lawrence's work (which has not usually been the case on the left since *Left Review*). He finds Lawrence revolutionary in outlook, astute in analysis, yet flawed in his approach to a solution. Spender recognises that, with his inconsistency and sometimes with mysticism, he could even be accommodated to Nazi philosophy, but that fundamentally he attacks the destruction of humane values in capitalist society. 'His denunciation of one institution at the very kernel of society was so true that it radiated outwards, exposing all the other institutions in its light.'

This contrasts with Douglas Garman's review of Lawrence's biography by Frieda Lawrence. Garman quickly moves from what Frieda wrote about her husband to a more general discussion of Lawrence, but, unlike Spender's critique, he is concerned primarily with what is wrong with Lawrence's social analysis. Garman insists on rational judgement, which is lacking in Lawrence's solution, whereas Spender finds Lawrence's encouragement to reject bourgeois values revolutionary.

Again, in reviewing *Ulysses*, Spender does not subscribe to what came to be the dominant Marxist critical view of Joyce, that he is simply decadent. Even though he finds no message in the novel, Spender thinks the form is itself a major achievement. He explains how Joyce relies on musical form and uses it to create significance.

Spender's reviewing of poetry brought him into opposition with more explicitly political criticism. In his review of five books of new poetry he properly gives prominence to poetic quality and technique (consistent with Day Lewis's warning early on that 'the first qualification of a poem is that it should be a good poem – technically good' – see Section II); but he *separates* it from the active political world by somewhat mystifying it – i.e. making it a quality beyond rational description – as in his comment that 'Irun's ruins' become 'part of Barker's spiritual habitation' and 'he is capable of imaginative experience to the degree to which it is only possible to the true poet'. Spender's critique raises the problem of how immediate the focus of criticism should be. His own sense of politics involves not just a political position but full personal integration and adjustment of social values, but sometimes this seems a little long-term for the political demands of the day. This placed Spender as a fine and sensitive critic but a bit too far behind the lines of action, and Douglas Garman offered a particular critique of Spender in reviewing *Writing in Revolt*, a collection of socialist critical essays, poems and stories. Spender, he said, claims the authority of Marxism but 'has as yet failed to apprehend either intellectually or imaginatively the significance of dialectical materialism'. He remains an idealist, insisting 'on a fundamental differentiation between The Poet and the rest of humanity' (III, 8: 499).

Revolutionary Art Criticism Argument

Revolutionary Art Criticism
[October 1935]
F. D. Klingender

Montagu Slater's review of Dimitri Tsapline's exhibition in the May issue of this publication raises the problem of the standard for revolutionary art criticism in so striking a manner that our return to it so long after the exhibition itself has been closed will, we hope, be excused. 'Sculpture, like some lyric poetry,' Slater writes, 'has to get near to the heart of things or it is nothing. *That is really what is at the back of the critics' formulae of recessions, planes and generalizations.*' Tsapline, we are told, 'beats the old world artists at their own game,' 'there are some archaic Greek lions in the British Museum which tell us all there is to know about one breed of lions. *Tsapline is almost on that level.*' Yet, according to Slater, Tsapline's London exhibition marks 'a step forward in our knowledge of what socialist art is going to look like!'

Let us assume that in making this latter claim he was thinking primarily of such pieces as the 'Workman,' the 'Guardian (U.S.S.R.),' or the 'Red Soldier' (illustrated in the May issue of the L.R.). These, we are told, are 'something which a sculptor from the other five-sixths of the world would not dream of being able to do.' They mean 'that Tsapline is finding a generalization for socialist life that holds good: holds good *in the sense that the generalizations of archaic Greek sculptures and the earlier Greek vases do.*'

Slater, it appears, consciously or unconsciously assumes that there is such a thing as art in the absolute aiming to get to the heart of 'things' by means of 'generalizing life.' Moreover its quality can, it seems, be assessed by such formal criteria as recessions, planes and generalizations, irrespective of its concrete class significance, one of its highest achievements being the art of archaic Greece. A slight modification of jargon and a healthy injection of enthusiasm thus appear to suffice in order to adapt the fashionable bourgeois critics' arsenal to the task of revolutionary art analysis. Let us examine the concrete results of this method.

Tsapline's career, the proud career of a Soviet peasant, soldier and artist until his departure from the U.S.S.R. in 1927, was quoted in Slater's review. By the time Tsapline was preparing to return to his country, eight years later, he had won the enthusiastic praise of bourgeois press reviewers both in Paris and London. It is natural for us as artists to ask: why? Was it because the tremendous experience of fighting for and actually building socialism in the Soviet Union and the contrast provided by his later experience of existence under Western Capitalism inspired a great artist to create masterpieces that swept the lifeless formalism of bourgeois art into insignificance? In other words, was Tsapline's success in bourgeois art circles due to the same causes as that of the great Soviet films? Tsapline's work exhibited in London ranged from molluscs and fish carved with only slight adaptations from water-washed rocks picked up at the seaside, to severely stylised heads and figures. There can be no doubt about this superb craftsmanship in the handling of the most varied and difficult materials. Yet it is remarkable that he is near to life, that he works from living experience and observation, *only* in the sphere most remote from our own (that of molluscs, etc.). His lions and other beasts of prey were unmistakably inspired by museum exhibits, not by life,[1] while in his approach to the problem that concerns us most, if not alone, he has lost all solid ground from beneath his feet and is left with the empty husk of mystical, idealized abstractions. Remove the Soviet Star from the helmet of the 'Red Soldier' (see May issue photograph) and you are left with a head that might have been taken straight from any one of a whole series of Bismarck towers and similar monuments of Wilhelmian Germany (e.g., Leipzig Völkerschlachtdenkmal). Or again, would any worker wielding a pneumatic drill eight hours a day feel the spark of personal experience if confronted with the cubist romanticism of Tsapline's 'Workman'?

The vitality of Tsapline's craftsmanship whenever he relies on his own resources makes it very doubtful whether Paris could have taught him much in the sphere of technique. But in the all-important sphere of content it did succeed in severing his roots from the mother soil of vital experience. Then the spectacle, from the bourgeois intellectual point of view 'interesting' and exciting, of a once illiterate peasant who has been provided by the Soviet Government with the possibility of artistic expression but unconsciously succumbed to the influences of bourgeois ideology during his protracted absence from the U.S.S.R. is the secret of Tsapline's success in the West. He must realize that these bourgeois ideologies are doomed, that they belong to the past and must be thrown overboard, if he is to save his great talent for the inspiring task of a Soviet artist.

Will Tsapline be helped in the painful recognition that from the alone important point of view the work of his last eight years was a failure, will he be helped in the heartrendingly difficult yet indispensable task of making a complete break, by reviews in revolutionary publications that join the bourgeois chorus of praise and shirk their duty of applying the only Marxian test of relevance to the problems of social reality? All art, even the most abstract, is socially relevant, has meaning in terms of the social reality in which it arose. But this relevance can be of a positive or a negative kind. Art can face the facts of social reality and point towards a method of their solution, or it can hide them and provide an escape from them. A third possibility is the open support of reaction at any given historical phase (feudal, imperialist, fascist, etc.). For the working class to-day only the first type has positive relevance, but it is clear that for the fascists, e.g., this is true of the third type, especially as it is accompanied by an apparent struggle against 'reaction' as represented by the second, 'art for art's sake' type of art.

There can be no doubt that whoever applies himself to revolutionary art criticism is shouldering a responsibility of quite exceptional gravity. For the problem of clarity, of breaking the shackles of bourgeois formalism, of penetrating to the roots of vital experience in the class struggle, and thus creating a truly revolutionary style, that problem is infinitely more difficult for our own artists than for those of the U.S.S.R. among whom the case of Tsapline is altogether exceptional. That is why any tendency – however deeply buried in the innermost recesses of the subconscious – of silently assuming that a Soviet artist 'can do no wrong' is the worst possible crime.

Marxian analysis cannot solve the problem of *creating* a revolutionary style out of the conditions of our own class reality – that is the task of the artist. But it can and must *prepare* the artist for this achievement by tearing him out of the dreamland of abstraction (the land of 'generalizations!') and bringing him face to face with his problem. This it can do by explaining the course of art development in terms of social fact, by irrefutably demonstrating to the artist that his present dilemma of form without content, the present apparent isolation of art from life, is the necessary outcome of a social reality (bourgeois existence in monopoly capitalism) that can no longer serve as a source for any genuine artistic experience. Moreover, once the point of abstract art is reached, as it is in this country to-day, once, that is to say, the artist *must* find a new content if he is to continue to work at all – for there is no such thing as form without content – the Marxian critic must convince him that only the class struggle pervading every sphere of our existence, only the aim of the working class to establish a new social order can enable him to find vital content for art to-day. Any return to the content of the past must lead to sterile reaction both socially and artistically.

That to achieve this aim of analysis the apparatus of bourgeois criticism is worse than useless goes without saying, for, more rapidly changing than the fashions of Paris, bourgeois aesthetic theory is on final analysis but the result of a conscious or unconscious attempt to hide the basic social roots of artistic experience. There can be only one standard for the assessment of any ideological phenomenon, whether of the present or of the past: its relevance in terms of social reality. More concretely speaking a revolutionary critic can only judge the *content* of art by the profundity of its social experience and its *form* by the degree to which it succeeds in transmitting the inspiring message of that experience to the working class and its allies.

Marx has taught us that because the ultimate result of their struggles was but the drab reality of bourgeois exploitation the revolutionaries of the seventeenth and eighteenth centuries were compelled to rely on a mythical past (Old Testament history or Republican Rome) as the source for their revolutionary enthusiasm. But he pointed out with no less insistence that the proletarian revolution must 'let the dead bury their dead,' that because its substance is the final liberation of mankind from all exploitation, it must create its art, its poetry, anew out of the future (opening pages of the

Eighteenth Brumaire). An inspiring task – but one requiring our best efforts and full concentration if we are to succeed.

Note

1. Assyrian and Egyptian animal carvings surely attracted him far more powerfully than archaic Greek ones. We can only grasp the implications of such a subjection to the influence of this or any other earlier style if we realize what that art or style meant in terms of its own social base. In this case the concrete content, the ideological significance of ancient animal carvings is not 'all there is to know about ... lions,' but the glorification of the god-king the despot whose superhuman strength in conquering the king of beasts served to impress his subjects: 'I am Asurbanipal, King of the World, King of Assyria. For my royal entertainment I grasped a desert lion by his tail. At the command of Nibib and Nergal, the gods, my guardians, I split his skull with a double edged sword,' is the inscription on one of the famous lion reliefs in the British Museum.

(II, 1: 38–40)

Montagu Slater's Reply [October 1935]

Montagu Slater writes: It is a pity neither my critics nor myself can go and have another look at Tsapline's work and check our reactions by the things themselves. He seems to have missed the normal meaning of the phrase 'something else is at the back of it.' Something else is at the back of the formulae planes and recessions as surely as Polonius was at the back of the arras. But there are several misunderstandings to which I hope to reply in the next number. In the meantime the article *The Turning Point*, in this issue, bears indirectly on the differences between us.

(II, 1: 40)

Abyssinian Methods [November 1935]
Ralph Fox

It was inevitable that sooner or later the left wing movement's Blimps and Bygadsbys should burst into the *Review*. Colonel Blimp-Klingender's little effort on 'Revolutionary Art Criticism' in last month's issue was a happy example of the heavy-handed, heavy-headed style of our old friends.

I am not personally in the least concerned whether or not Dimitri Tsapline is a good sculptor. At least if he reads the sound advice given him by our English revolutionary art critic he will understand he has got to do better in future and will feel duly sorry for having done so badly in the past. Mr. Klingender is sure that the best way to 'help' Tsapline is to tell him he is a misguided bourgeois with a very, very naughty tendency towards carving molluscs and fishes. I am sure the best way to help Mr. Klingender would be to deprive him of pen and ink for the rest of his life. But others, of course, may think differently, some that this would be too harsh, others that it would not be half harsh enough.

While sympathizing with the latter, I must point out to them that perhaps the best way to treat someone who solemnly writes about there being 'only one standard for the assessment of any ideological phenomenon, whether of the present or the past: its relevance in terms of social reality,' is simply to take away his writing licence for life, rather than resort to more Abyssinian forms of punishment.

All art, says our Blimp, even the most abstract, is socially relevant, has meaning in terms of the social reality in which it arose. Dear, dear, shades of Courthope and other good old materialists! We may agree to this very clear statement of the obvious, but what has it to do with Marxism? What has it to do with art, or criticism?

With all the ardour of a youthful Columbus burning to tell us of his new America and smack us over the knuckles for not being equally thrilled, Mr Klingender goes on to expand his remarkable canons of art criticism. Art, it seems, can face social reality, or it can hide from it, or it can support reaction. If it is bold enough to face social reality, that is not enough, for it must also 'point towards a method of solution.'

It is all very old-fashioned and charming, but what it has to do with Marxism, I fail to see. John Ruskin and his moral theories of art, yes, or even the liberal humanitarians of the same period, but Marxism, Mr. Klingender, never, never, never.

Where in all this conception is dialectic? In this horrible jumble of rigid moral and sociological conceptions, where is the idea of inner development, where the real connection between form and content? A 'revolutionary' critic can 'only judge the *content* of art by the profundity of its social experience and its *form* by the degree to which it succeeds in transmitting the inspiring message of that experience to the working-class and its allies.'

So Mr. Klingender judges the formal question of whether or not a work of art is beautiful, by the *moral* test of the degree in which it succeeds in making 'the working class and its allies' shout a fervent 'Red Front,' though I cannot but suspect that when Mr. K. writes 'working class and its allies' he has in mind nobody else but Mr. K. without allies.

Suppose, for a moment, the unthinkable thing. An artist produces a work which actually arouses admiration in the enemies of the working class, as well as among workers 'and their allies' – how would our revolutionary critic explain it? But what puzzles me even more, how does he apply this criterion to the art of the past?

The greatest artistic event of our generation in England, the exhibition of Chinese art, is about to open. Will our critic take his pupils to this display of the supreme artistic genius of all time and explain to them carefully that the Chinese artists and craftsmen were only the representatives of a decayed and rotten feudalism and that very often they sought to escape from the rather unpleasant facts of Chinese social reality, and sometimes they even supported the reactionary elements in that reality, so that we have really nothing to learn from them, because they transmit no inspiring 'Red Fronts' to us? Moreover, to make things worse, most of them drank too much.

If so, I am afraid his pupils will be reduced to tears, tears of boredom mingling with the tears shed for the moral decadence of the wretched Chinese.

It is hardly possible here to go into the very difficult and complex questions of Marxian aesthetics and criticism. The founders of scientific communism, though they read enormously in the literature of aesthetics and criticism, did not develop their ideas in any special works. Marx intended to do so, but never found the time. In all their books, and especially in their correspondence we can, however, find fruitful ideas and brilliant generalizations scattered abundantly, the foundation for a real Marxian art criticism.

How, Mr. Klingender, do you square your statement that 'Art can face the facts of social reality and point towards a method of their solution' with Engels' famous advice to a realist socialist novelist that 'the more the opinions of the author remain hidden, the better for the work of art. The realism I allude to, may crop out even in spite of the author.' Or again, in his letter to another socialist novelist, 'that the tendency (of a novel) should arise out of the situation and action itself without particularly pointing it out and the author is not compelled to bring to the reader a ready-made historical and future solution for the social conflicts he represents.' Indeed Engels goes further, and suggests that the author, provided he has painted a true picture of social and personal relations in his novel, need not even take sides. Yet such a timid author Engels would call 'socialist,' while Klingender would call him – something much more complicated, moral and obscure.

Or again, let us take Marx's criticism of Lassalle's revolutionary drama on the German wars of religion. It was full of inspiring messages, yet Marx had the audacity to suggest to him that a little less revolutionary inspiration and a little more art, would much improve it. 'Of course the ideological content must suffer, but that is inevitable, and the complete merging of a great ideological depth, a conscious historical content ... with Shakespearean liveliness, richness of action, will only no doubt be reached in the future.'

Marx's favourite novelist was Balzac. But strangely enough his favourite novel of Balzac's was not one in which the social background was the strongest feature. He was most deeply moved by a little book which Mr. Klingender has probably never read, *Le Chef d'Oeuvre Inconnu*. When he has read it I would be interested to see him applying his canons of 'revolutionary' and 'Marxist' criticism to this beautiful book.

(II, 2: 81–2)

[Review of] *Literature,*
Philip Henderson. [October 1935]
Edgell Rickword

With the stated intention of tracing 'the development of literature in relation to the social order of which it is always and everywhere the outcome,' Philip Henderson runs through English literature in 180 pages and contrives to include as well chapters on The Ancient World and on the Future. This is an overbold attempt, due rather to excess of enthusiasm than to pretentiousness. His book contains much vigorous indignation and some keen analysis of contemporary writers; but there are unfortunate omissions and frequent failures in his attempts to characterize the classic writers in the few lines he has available. More serious than these incidental defects is the fact that, in my opinion, the book would never convince anyone who was in doubt that literature really is the outcome of the social order. The response of such a person is much more likely to be 'Here's one of those dogmatic blokes again,' and there is some justification for it, one feels, reading such a mechanical formulation as this on Milton:

> 'Coming of a well-to-do middle-class family, he sums up in himself the by-now-powerful and independent spirit of his class.'

This has already been said, more concretely, by Taine, by Cazamian, by many modern academic critics who accept the notion that a writer expresses in some way his historical environment. But it is not specifically Marxist.

And when Henderson says 'a fuller exposition of the general standpoint implicit in this book will be found in' – *Anti-Duhring*, the very opposite is the truth. Henderson has revolted against the bourgeois mentality but he is still thinking abstractly, metaphysically. Society was feudal, it became bourgeois, it is going to be socialist – so much he knows; but of the interplay of these classes, the dialectical relationship between them, which is the law of humanity in motion, he realizes nothing, or at any rate does not apply it to the subject matter in front of him.

'Unfortunately, the brilliance of the Elizabethan period was only a surface gloss. "There are paupers everywhere," exclaimed the Queen after a journey through her realm' – this effective quotation gives the measure of his indictment, repeated for different centuries, of bourgeois literature. It contains some fine achievements but – what about the wretched poor? Such an attitude gets us no further than humanitarianism, an age-old sentiment reaching at its farthest utopian socialism, and certainly a factor in the disintegration of the bourgeois ideology, but powerless in the absence of a revolutionary class theory. The misery and destitution of some layers of the population, though at times reaching the pitch of revolt, could not provide the motive power for a successful revolution till the struggles of the very class whose achievements Henderson so cursorily dismisses had provided an adequate material basis.

The significant relation is not between rich and poor, but between the progressive and obstructive classes, between the class that is expanding the productive capacity and that of those which are fettering it. For instance the centralization of feudalism was progressive in relation to the tribal communities of the Heroic Age in Northern Europe. And since Henderson mentions Marlowe and his boyishly exuberant *Tamburlain* with its glorification of wealth and worldly power, he should also have mentioned *Dr. Faustus*, whose infinite intellectual ambition sought its consummation in 'magic,' that is in realms of knowledge forbidden by clerical authority. That was surely an anticipation of what Francis Bacon was to initiate a few years later by 'laying the foundations of inductive thinking' – which is all the acknowledgment he gets in this book. But if 'Electrification plus Soviet power equals communism,' are not the foundations of inductive thinking the pre-requisite for communism?

To return to Marlowe. Even in the gold, pearls and blood orgies of *Tamburlain* there is this passage:

Our soul, whose faculties can comprehend
The wondrous architecture of the world:
And measures every wandering planet's course,
Still climbing after knowledge infinite
And always moving as the restless spheres
Wills us to wear ourselves and never rest....

These lines seem to me to express an emotion that is far from being incompatible with dialectical materialism, though it is incompatible with the philosophies that are flourishing under monopoly capitalism, with its frustration of the scientific impulse.[1]

It may be remembered, too, that Marlowe formulated in a primitive form the materialist conception of religion. In the report of the police spy who took down some conversation of his, it is stated that Marlowe tried to persuade people not to be afraid of 'bugbears and hobgoblins' and that he said 'The first beginning of religion was only to keep men in awe.'

The eighteenth century with its self-complacency and respect for formality wins little praise from our author. Yet the distaste for fanaticism, the striving for a rational explanation of phenomena and the substitution of humanistic for theological values which is the content of its fiction and its not very enthralling verse, was all part of a long process of emancipation. Yet we are hurried impatiently through it till we come to Burns, when we are told 'it is once more to the *working-class* that we must turn for any genuine feeling.' This is the first we have heard of the working-class since the ballad literature was mentioned some hundreds of years before; but it is to very little of that, even, that *working-class* can be applied in any real sense. And is it not very short sighted to confine the term 'genuine feeling' to certain kinds of emotion? Is not the feeling in Gibbon's *Decline and Fall of the Roman Empire* genuine? And was not this a valuable work, in its setting up of a standard of historical objectivity against the monkish obscurantism of the church interests? The violence of the attacks on it are proof of that. But it is not even mentioned here. Besides, up to this time the great majority of what Henderson calls the working-class were small-scale producers and one of their representative books, written by a hell-haunted tinker, Bunyan, was *The Pilgrim's Progress*. This, a best-seller of all time, is not mentioned either.

It was a trait of our Georgian poets to associate genuine feeling with agricultural activities, a delusion which Henderson seems to share with them:

'Only Burns, who spent his life in touch with the primal things of man's existence, who sowed and reaped with his own hands the very bread he ate, could have written such a poem as that *To a Mouse, on turning her up in her nest with the plough, November 1785*, with a tenderness that was real and not affected. One shudders to think of the same subject treated by Goldsmith, for instance.'

It is unfortunate that Goldsmith should be picked on here, because he wrote a poem expressing, with genuine feeling, it seems to me, a sense of the tragedy and injustice of the enclosures as complete as our critic's own. *The Deserted Village* is an unequivocal indictment of the greed of the wealthy, and if the formality of its language is proof that its emotions are unreal and affected, then there is very little genuine feeling in art at all.

Where then, ah! where, shall poverty reside
To 'scape the pressure of contiguous pride?
If to some common's fenceless limit strayed,
He drives his flock to pick the scanty blade,
Those fenceless fields the sons of wealth divide,
And even the bare-worn common is denied.

There is better poetry in the poem than that, but those lines are enough to show that though Goldsmith did not plough the land he was not indifferent to human suffering, and is in agreement with Henderson in his sympathy with expropriated peasants. But what was the only possible reaction, pity and indignation, for a humane man in 1770, is not the only, nor the most essential one, at this later date.

As our intellectual understanding of society is developed, our emotional habits cannot but be re-cast. The understanding of this peasant problem which Engels already showed in *The Condition of the Working Class in 1844* is further developed in this passage from *The Housing Question*:

'In order to create the modern revolutionary class of the proletariat it was absolutely necessary to cut the umbilical cord which still bound the worker of the past to the land. The hand weaver, in his little house, garden and field, along with his loom, was a "quiet contented man in all godliness and respectability," despite all misery and all political pressure; he doffed his cap to the rich, to the priests and to the officials of the state, and inwardly was altogether a slave.' In spite of the undoubted worsening of the workers' material situation, 'the English proletarian of 1872 is on an infinitely higher level than the rural weaver of 1772 with his "hearth and home".'

And so no doubt would Burns have agreed, ploughing his own land amongst kirk-scared hypocrites also ploughing their own land but as resentful of the 'genuine feelings' he expressed as any town bourgeois. At any rate Burns lashed them in his satire.

If the evil effects of the separation of intellectual from manual labour were to be understood as simply as that, then the sooner we get back to small individual production the better.

When Henderson contrasts 'the sterile intellectualism' of the 'cultured' classes, at the end of the eighteenth century with the lyricism of Burns he has got his chronology wrong and he should have kept his contemptuous quotation marks for another hundred years or so. ... The working-class was only just coming into existence as a class. It quickly began to take form, and its interests, together with those of the industrial bourgeoisie and the landed aristocracy, further complicated the ideological superstructure. An example of this, where the antagonisms between the two older classes favoured the younger class, is missed at this point – the case of Byron. Henderson dismisses Byron as a romantic egoist wandering sombrely over the Continent. Yet there are at any rate three aspects of Byron which compel a reconsideration of this limited view of him and his work.

(1) His speech in the House of Lords on the death penalty being applied to machine wreckers, in 1812:

> 'These men never destroyed their looms till they were become useless; till they were become actual impediments to their exertions in earning their daily bread. Can you, then, wonder that in times like these, when bankruptcy convicted fraud and felony are found in a station not far beneath that of your lordships, the lowest, though once the most useful portion of the people, should forget their duty in their distresses and become only less guilty than one of repre-

sentatives? But while the exalted offender can find means to baffle the law....'

Do we hear that tone from our Labour lords – about the Blaina riot and sentences, for instance?

(2) Byron died as a result of his efforts to assist the Greeks in their struggle for national independence.

That, in the historical circumstances, was a definitely progressive rôle.

(3) He wrote *Don Juan*, where mockery of the brutality and hypocrisy of the ruling classes was given free play. No doubt the reason for its comparative neglect by official critics.

As Marx said 'The greater the development of the antagonisms between the growing forces of production and the extant social order, the more does the ideology of the ruling class become permeated with hypocrisy,' a fact which explains the popular association of intensified puritanism with the accession of Queen Victoria. That the progressive rôle of the class was dwindling is seen in the decline in seriousness in literature, though science was not so soon stultified. Henderson refers to Darwin as 'preaching Natural Selection, the Survival of the Fittest and the Devil take the hindermost.'

But competition was preached as the golden rule by the industrial bourgeoisie before Darwin wrote, and though they sought some support from his theory, on the whole the Victorians were hostile to the new discovery – and well they might be. For Marx, a year after the publication of the *Origin of Species* wrote:

'Darwin's book is very important and serves me as a basis in natural science for the class struggle in history. Despite all deficiencies, not only is the death-blow dealt for the first time to "teleology" in the natural sciences but their rational meaning is empirically explained.'

Such lapses are not trivial, they are due to a mistaken approach to the subject, and specifically, to the failure to set the writers dealt with in their concrete historical environment, which may differ even for contemporaries in the same political unit, e.g., for Burns and Goldsmith. It is to their class affiliation that we must look for the understanding of writers, and this is naturally essential in our present-day, when so many writers feel the division in themselves which operates in society, whilst unable for a time to see the necessity of taking part in the progressive movement. That is one of the reasons why we must be on guard against the schematic classification of bourgeois literature into which the author of this book so often falls.

(II, 1: 41–4)

1. Rickword captures Marlowe's image perfectly but misquotes in detail and spells Tamburlaine idiosyncratically, which suggests that he is working from memory; he is making a cultural argument rather than constructing a literary 'proof'.

The German Drama: Pre-Hitler

[July 1936]

Bert Brecht

[Bert Brecht, now visiting England, is known as one of the most brilliant contributors to the flourishing period of theatrical experiment in post-war Berlin. His best-known work is in the operettas 'Mahoganny' and 'Die Dreigroschenoper' (Beggars' Opera). His influence has been strong on the development of young English poets and playwrights such as W. H. Auden.]

The years after the World War saw the German theatre in a period of a great flowering. We had more great actors than at any other time. There were quite a number of prominent régisseurs, or directors, such as Reinhardt, Jessner, Engel, and so on, who competed sharply and interestingly with one another. Almost all plays of world literature, from *Oedipus* to *Les Affaires Sont Les Affaires*, from the Chinese *Chalk Circle* to Strindberg's *Fräulein Julia*, could be played. And they were played.

Nevertheless, for us young people the theatre had one serious flaw. Neither its highly developed stage technique nor its dramaturgy permitted us to present on the stage the great themes of our times; as, for example, the building-up of a mammoth industry, the conflict of classes, war, the fight against disease, and so on. These things could not be presented, at least not in an adequate manner. Of course, a stock exchange could be, and was, shown on the stage, or trenches, or clinics. But they formed nothing but effective background for a sort of sentimental 'magazine story' that could have taken place at any other time, though in the great periods of the theatre they would not have been found worthy of being shown on the stage. The development of the theatre so that it could master the presentation of modern events and themes, and overcome the problems of showing them, was brought about only with great labour.

One thing that helped solve the problem was the 'electrification' of the mechanics of staging plays. Within a few years after this problem of developing the modern stage had made itself felt among us, Piscator, who without doubt is one of the most important theatre men of all times, began to transform its scenic potentialities. He introduced a number of far-reaching innovations.

One of them was his use of the film and of film projections as an integral part of the settings. The setting was thus awakened to life and began to play on its own, so to speak; the film was a new, gigantic actor that helped to narrate events. By means of it documents could be shown as part of the scenic background, figures and statistics. Simultaneous events in different places could be seen together. For example, while a fight was going on between two characters for the possession of an Albanian oil field, one could see on the screen in the background warships being launched in preparation for putting that oil field out of commission entirely.

This was great progress. Another innovation was the introduction of moving platforms on the stage. On these moving bands that traversed the stage we played, for example, *Brave Soldier Schweik* and his famous march to Budweis, which took a half-hour and which was made great and entertaining by the actor Max Pfallenberg. Pfallenberg had to leave Germany at the beginning of the Third Reich and has since died. The elevator-stage on which the *Merchants of Berlin* was performed made vertical action on the stage possible. New facilities for staging allowed the use of musical and graphic elements which the theatre up to this time had not been able to employ. These inspired composers of rank to write music for the theatre. The great cartoonist George Grosz made valuable contributions for the projections. His drawings for the performance of *Schweik* have been published by the Malik Press in Berlin.

We made many experiments. I can tell of some of my own work, as I know that best. We organised small collectives of specialists in various fields to 'make' the plays; among these specialists were historians and sociologists as well as playwrights, actors and other people of the theatre. I had begun to work upon theories and experiments in a non-Aristotelian drama. Some of the theories I have put down in fragments in the seven volumes of 'Versuche' (English translation, *Experiments*), which were published by the Gustav Kieperheil Press in Berlin. This dramaturgy does not make use of the 'identification' of the spectator with the play, as the Aristotelian, and has a different point of view also toward other psychological effects a play may have on an audience, as, for example, toward the 'catharsis.' Catharsis is not the main object of this dramaturgy.

It does not make the hero the victim of an inevitable fate, nor does it wish to make the spectator the victim, so to speak, of a hypnotic experience in the theatre. In fact, it has as a purpose the 'teaching' of the spectator a certain quite practical attitude; we have to make it possible for him to take a critical attitude while he is in the theatre (as opposed to a subjective attitude of becoming completely 'entangled' in what is going on). Some of my plays of this type of dramaturgy are *St. Joan of the Stockyards*, *Mann ist Mann*, and *Round Heads and Pointed Heads*.

The non-Aristotelian dramaturgy investigated also the field of the opera. One result of this investigation was the opera *The Rise and Fall of the City of Mahoganny*, which I wrote and to which Kurt Weill wrote the music. Theoretical comments concerning this opera may be found in the second volume of the *Versuche*. Another was the *Dreigroschenoper*, *Three-penny Opera*, which, again, I wrote with Weill.

At the same time, the training of a whole generation of young actors for the new style of acting, the epic style, took place. Many of these worked with us in various theatres in Berlin. The beginning of the Third Reich scattered these actors all over the world. Oskar Homolka and Fritz Kortner are in London, Carla Neher is in Moscow, and so are Alexander Granach and Ernst Busch. Helene Weigel is in Copenhagen, Peter Lorre is in Hollywood and London, Lotte Lenya (Mrs. Kurt Weill) is in Zurich, and, I hear, will soon be in New York. Some of them played in the Berlin production of *Mother*.

At this time, too, another series of experiments that made use of theatrical effects but that often did not need the stage in the old sense was undertaken and led to certain results. These led to the 'lehrstuecke,' for which the nearest English equivalent I can find is the 'learning-play.'[1]

Mother is such a learning-play, and embodies certain principles and methods of presentation of the non-Aristotelian, or epic style, as I have sometimes called it; the use of the film projection to help bring the social complex of the events taking place to the forefront; the use of music and of the chorus to supplement and vivify the action on the stage; the setting forth of actions so as to call for a critical approach, so that they would not be taken for granted by the spectator and would arouse him to think; it became obvious to him which were right actions and which were wrong ones.

Briefly, the Aristotelian play is essentially static; its task is to show the world as it is. The learning-play is essentially dynamic; its task is to show the world as it changes (and also how it may be changed). It is a common truism among the producers and writers of the former type of play that the audience, once it is in the theatre, is not a number of individuals but a collective individual, a mob, which must be and can be reached only through its emotions; that it has the mental immaturity and the high emotional suggestibility of a mob. We have often seen this pointed out in treatises on the writing and production of plays. The latter theatre holds that the audience is a collection of individuals, capable of thinking and of reasoning, of making judgments even in the theatre; it treats it as individuals of mental and emotional maturity, and believes it wishes to be so regarded.

With the learning-play, then, the stage begins to be didactic. (A word of which I, as a man of many years of experience in the theatre, am not afraid.) The theatre becomes a place for philosophers, and for such philosophers as not only wish to explain the world but wish to change it.

Thus there is philosophy, thus there is instruction – but where is the fun? Are we to be put again on the school bench, and treated as learners of our ABCs? Are we supposed to pass examinations and work for credits? It is generally thought that there is a great difference between learning and having fun. The first may be useful, but only the latter is agreeable. I therefore have to defend this theatre against the suspicion that it is a humourless, yes, even awfully strenuous affair. Well, I can only say to that that there is not necessarily a difference between learning and having fun. Doubtless the sort of learning which we remember from our school days, from all those preparations for professions, is a most toilsome, wearying affair. But there is a learning that is full of joy, full of fun, a militant learning.

If there were not such entertaining learning, then the entire theatre would not be able to instruct. For theatre remains theatre even while it is didactic, and as long as it is good theatre it is also entertaining. In Germany, philosophers discussed these learning-plays, and plain people saw them and enjoyed them, and also discussed them.

I learned from these discussions. I feel myself I must still, must always, learn. From what I learned from the audiences that saw it, I rewrote *Mann ist Mann* ten times, and presented it at different times in different ways – for example, in Darmstadt in 1926, at the Berlin Volksbuehne in 1927, at the Berlin Federal Theatre in 1929.

For some years, in carrying out my experiments, I tried, with a small staff of collaborators, to work outside the theatre, which, having for so long been forced to 'sell' an evening's entertainment, had retreated into too inflexible limits for such experiments; we tried a type of theatrical performance that could influence the thinking of all the people engaged in it. We worked with different means and in different strata of society. These experiments were theatrical performances meant not so much for the spectator as for those who were engaged in the performance. It was, so to speak, art for the producer, not art for the consumer.

I wrote, for example, plays for schools, and small operas. The *Ja-Sager* was one of them. These plays could be performed by students. Another of these plays was *The Flight of the Lindberghs*, a play that called for the collaboration of the schools with the radio. The radio broadcast into the schools the accompanying orchestral music and solo parts, while the classes in the schools sang the choruses and did the minor rôles. For this piece Hindemith and Weill wrote music. It was done at the Baden-Baden Music Festival in 1929. The Baden learning-play, *Experiment No. 7*, is for men and women choruses, and uses also the film and clowns as performers. The music is by Hindemith. Experiment No. 12 was a learning-play, *Expedient*. Several workers' choruses joined in performing it. The chorus consisted of 400 singers, while several prominent actors played the solo parts. The music was by Hanns Eisler.

I might add that the experiments that we undertook at the Nollendorf Theatre and at the Schiffbauerdamm Theatre alone cost more than half a million dollars, though some plays, like *Schweik*, had continuous runs of more than six months, and the *Three-Penny Opera* played for more than a year continuously, so much time and money indeed did the special machinery and the dramaturgical laboratories for these experiments need.

Note

1. Since Brecht's works are practically unobtainable in published form,
    all available copies having been burnt by the Nazis, some further
    elucidation of what he means by non-Aristotelian or 'Epic' drama may
    be appended here. Brecht wishes both actor and audience to stand
    outside the character and incidents portrayed on the stage. The actor is
    to feel himself not overflowing with the real emotions of a Hamlet or a
    Lear, but reproducing them, portraying them, while retaining his own
    independence as commentator and observer. Similarly, the spectator
    retains his right to criticise Hamlet or Lear, and not to be swept away
    in the flood of emotions which the poet has generated around those
    characters. In the appendix to *Mahoganny* – Kurt Weill's opera for
    which Brecht wrote the libretto – the following contrast is made:

Dramatic style	*Epic style*
involves the spectator in action on the stage and	forces the spectator to consider action on the stage but
consumes his activity.	wakes his activity.
gives him sensations.	compels him to come to decisions.
Suggestion.	Argument.
Excitement as to the dénouement.	Excitement as to the course of the action.
One scene for the others.	Each scene for itself.
Growth.	Montage.
Feeling.	Ratio.

(II, 10: 504–8)

Surrealism Argument

Surrealism and Revolutions[1] [January 1937]
A. L. Lloyd

We need a revolution in consciousness, liberation of the imagination, say the Surrealists, and take as their motto Lautréamont's dictum that 'Poetry should be made by everybody and not by one.' To summarise their standpoint we may say they believe that the human mind possesses a powerful lyrical capacity which is, as a rule, more or less overlaid by more immediate conscious and rational necessities. There are occasions when this lyrical element emerges, when we are made aware of the tremendous potentialities of the mind of *every* human being. So far, because of the lack of systematisation of this element, we see its emergence most clearly in dream, delirium, and pathological obsession (e.g. paranoia). But since the mind, under these latter circumstances, is sick, the delirious image is inevitably distorted accordingly, and assumes proportions of terror. However, it is essential to remember that in health, too, the mind retains that capacity but submerged, only waiting to be exploited. The form of these lyrical bases is common to all people, from millionaire to dustman, from London to Hong Kong. The Surrealists claim that the exploitation of this capacity, common to all, even the most primitive, the most backward, means the destruction of the old bourgeois fable of the 'Genius.'

So, for the Surrealists, the old views of art are ruled out, the constructive intelligence banished, and they endeavour to revolutionise consciousness by disregarding as far as possible the intellectual and emotional layers of the mind, and by concentrating on the deep unconscious layers, such as come to the surface in dream, delirium and delusion. 'It is necessary to act,' said Goethe. 'It is necessary to dream,' said Lenin. Surrealists claim their activity is the dialectical resolution of these antitheses, action and dream, logical necessity and natural necessity, objectivity and subjectivity. Their special revolutionary annexe, they declare, is to break down the inhibitions, the sordid repressive apparatus, deliberately fostered by certain bourgeois institutions, such as patriotism, religion, the family, etc. These inhibitions, they rightly claim, being irrational, are not to be broken down by mere appeals to reason, and stereotyped declarations against Fascism and war, etc., whether those declarations be in the form of speeches, literature or painting.

Now it is true that, as M. Breton has remarked, ethically, psychologically, polemical art explains nothing, except superficially. Exterior facts it shows, interior facts not at all.

In the history of bourgeois art proper there has always been two currents, conformative art (closely bound to the dominant class) and nonconformative art. The latter is not necessarily immediately social and polemical, like the work of Daumier. M. Breton rightly says: 'To put forward his name is to simplify the problem, to give too much importance to one solution, satire.' For also non-conformative are Baudelaire, Rimbaud and particularly Courbet and Seurat. We all know how sad it is to see politically left artists preoccupied with painting academic pictures of muscle-bound workers with a hammer and sickle appearing in the sky above them, or of *Daily Worker* canvassers in action.

Let us then consider how the revolutionary artist should work. 'Take Courbet, for example,' the Surrealists say (though with unusual modesty they don't claim him as one of themselves), 'Courbet was an active revolutionary, a member of the Commune. He ordered the destruction of the Colonne Vendôme, monument to Napoleon's victories, in the face of an angry flood of anonymous letters, signed "Survivor of Austerlitz," etc. He painted forests, women, the sea, still-lives. Most of his themes were not different from those of the other painters of his time. There is little trace – in his subject-matter – of his active social preoccupations. He did not choose to paint the episodes of the great revolutionary movement in which he took part.' More's the pity, no doubt. Anyone who is familiar with the hysterical and vicious attacks on Courbet which were conducted in the powerful French comic papers of the time, will have noticed that Courbet's work affronted the ruling class by the sole virtue of its implications. Despite his ostracism by the art critics, his influence has so spread that it is no exaggeration to say that modern painting would have been otherwise had Courbet not lived.

'Here,' the Surrealists say, 'we have the case of a man with proven sensibility caught up in some of the most striking circumstances in history. These circumstances led him to state his convictions implicitly, not to give an immediately polemical sense to his art. In the same way, implicitly that is to say, we too are revolutionaries though we are not usually propagandists.' Because Courbet was a revolutionary painter, they claim that so, too, are Picasso and Max Ernst. 'Think of Picasso's "Meurtre de Marat",' they say, 'or Ernst's "La Révolution la Nuit".'

But, alas, it is not possible to admit that these are revolutionary artists in any practical, political sense, for the very good reason that, unlike the implications of Courbet, the underlying message of their work is not conducive to social or revolutionary responsibility. For while Courbet, in every line that he painted, is *materialist, fearless*, and *practical* – and therein lies his great revolutionary efficiency as an artist – Picasso, Ernst and their colleagues, however sensitive their work may be, however aesthetically excellent, are *metaphysical, fearful*, and *irresponsible*. The work of Courbet is, in its implications, as sensible as a Pollitt speech. Whereas Picasso, in his works, is not a revolutionary at all, his paintings are but symptoms of a state of things of which revolution can be the only outcome.

Meanwhile, just when the people of Spain are fighting for their lives and their liberty, M. Breton decides that the time is ripe for another round of Soviet-baiting. While his Catalan compatriots die in their thousands, fighting against Fascism, M. Dali trips off to Italy to sell his pictures to wealthy supporters of Mussolini – not neglecting, however, to cash in on his compatriots' struggle by *renaming*, a little late in the day, one of his most monstrously melodramatic works, with the title of 'Spain – Premonitions of the Civil War,' an unpleasant act of downright fraud which serves to illustrate the fake metaphysics which so often stigmatises the work of this particular gentleman and his friends.

The fact is the Surrealists deceive themselves. The bourgeois intelligentsia as a whole deplores the mass spirit as it understands it, its members resent the monotony and uniformity of their own lives. They have a pitiful tendency to pursue the phantom of whatever is picturesque and exotic (they *must* see Belmonte before they die!), the depths of dream life and the unconscious cast them into ecstasies, they are enchanted with any little originality, however superficial. The Surrealist is caught in the trap of individualism in this way: try as he may, he can do no more than sublimate the narcissism of the bourgeoisie, the ideas they have about their own bodies, their own desires, their own individuality, their own thoughts (so that at last they begin to imagine they are only thinking importantly when they are thinking irrationally. Then they can be sure they are thinking their *own* thoughts!).

In a society divided into classes in which the individual has no very precise realisation of his rôle, the more limited, more passive beings will try to explain and justify their existence by a central pathetic idea, a kind of discreet interior lyricism by which individuals may amplify their daily actions and no question of physical risk is involved *nor any real action of social consequence.*

If Surrealism were revolutionary, it could be of use. But Surrealism is not revolutionary, because its lyricism is socially irresponsible. It does not lead fantasy into any action of real social significance. Surrealism is a particularly subtle form of fake revolution. It has no bearing on proletarian problems, gives no twist towards social responsibility. No doubt the leaders of the Surrealist movement do not realise it is all a fake. They are often very innocent people. Actually it seems the significance of Surrealism in the political field is at present rather counter-revolutionary than otherwise. Individuals and masses are only passive, inasmuch as they have illusory consciousness of activity within the frame of the bourgeoisie, *individual* activity. It is not until they realise that this freedom, this semblance of activity and of significance is an illusion that the starting point is provided for the formation of active masses and the development of a revolutionary consciousness.

And, despite what the Surrealists may say, all this involves *reason.* Of course, we know that reason alone never decided a man to act, but in the face of the Surrealist tendency to discredit the intellect, one must remember John Strachey's words: 'You cannot begin to find any rational explanation of why corn is being burnt in one place while people are starving for it in another. The mind rebels against such a situation. And the rebellion of a man's mind is the beginning, though only the beginning, of the revolution of the whole man. We begin to see why it is necessary for the

Fascists, whose object it is to perpetuate our more and more irrational capitalist system, to assail in every conceivable way the supremacy of human reason.'

Quite obviously the Surrealists, particularly the English group, who have already issued an admirable proclamation calling for 'Arms for the people of Spain,' and have collected a considerable sum of money for the support of the Spanish Government, have no sort of Fascist motives behind their work. It may even be that the Surrealist movement does bring over to the working-class movement certain of the potentially Fascist middle classes. And that is very good. But for them to claim revolutionary activity beyond that is, I feel, a piece of self-deception. The revolutionary is not made by fraudulent conversion. And that he can only become real and effective through class and mass is a platitude which is none the less true. These frivolous games of automatism and newspaper-clipping-creation, of goosy ghost-hunting and a hazardous preoccupation with chance, though in many cases of undoubted scientific interest and value, can play no serious part in making the proletariat conscious of its social and revolutionary responsibilities.

Note

1. *Surrealism*, edited by Herbert Read. *Faber and Faber*: 12s. 6d.

(II, 16: 895–8)

Herbert Read and Hugh Sykes Davies Reply
[February 1937]

Mr. Lloyd repeats the old criticism that Surrealism is irrational and anti-rational, but in such a profitable form that he deserves a reply.

It is true that we believe 'the human mind possesses a powerful lyrical capacity which is overlaid by immediate conscious and rational necessities.' We also believe (and here Mr. Lloyd has not quite understood us) that this lyrical impulse has often expressed itself and continues to express itself not in isolation, but in combination with other impulses and other kinds of human activity. In much poetry, for example in Milton, Wordsworth, Tennyson, Browning, it is combined with religious feeling and dogma; and there is a strikingly large lyrical element in most idealist philosophy. Now, whatever may have been the effects of such a combination in the past, we are convinced that at present it is extremely dangerous to allow the lyrical element to combine with our intellectual positions. Our interest in the lyrical impulse is motivated, certainly, by our belief in its importance; but it is motivated no less by our belief that if it is not isolated, studied, and brought under rational control, it will remain a source of danger to our reason. For the moment, then, we isolate the lyrical impulse, not because we are anti-rational, but because we wish to preserve a clear reason. If we have intellectual positions to explain, we shall explain them in the most direct, the most rational, the least lyrical form possible to us.

'Lyrical.' We have used the word because Mr. Lloyd puts it into our mouths. But in doing so he misrepresents us a little more. It is obviously a word which belongs entirely to the bourgeois game of literary criticism, and has no meaning outside the rules of that game. Further, it is intimately connected with notions of inspiration, and so with religious and idealistic assumptions: traditionally the lyrical product is held to be inexplicable in material terms, and so to be a proof of the existence of 'something beyond matter,' 'the divine element in human personality,' and so forth. We have found it necessary to step outside the bounds of bourgeois criticism, and to study the 'lyrical impulse' not from a literary point of view, but from the point of view of general psychology, taking evidence from mental disease, other abnormal conditions, from anthropology, and from actual experiment. It is obviously impossible to say that we are studying the 'lyrical impulse,' since we have moved so far from the categories to which that word belongs. Our own word for the subject of our study, dream-activity, is by no means free from objections, but it at least indicates that our approach is not literary-critical.

As for the 'social irresponsibility' of our 'lyricism,' of which Mr. Lloyd complains pointedly, we can only ask for time. We are only at the beginning of our work, and we must admit that to many problems we have as yet no sort of an answer. But we are as conscious as Mr. Lloyd himself that one of our main concerns must be with the development of a socially responsible lyrical tendency, though we may come to conceive it differently from what he would wish.

In the meantime, we know that socially responsible lyricism will never come from socially irresponsible personalities, and we are grateful to Mr. Lloyd for recognising the fact that we are socially active. We must agree with him in all that he says concerning the behaviour of other Surrealists. Where Dali was concerned, we were most of us pretty fly already. But, on the other hand, Benjamin Peret has been working in Spain almost from the beginning of the war, and two members of the English group have worked in Barcelona for some time. We are also concerned, individually and collectively, in various other activities connected with Spain and with the English political situation. We shall continue to co-operate to the fullest extent in all revolutionary activity to which we can contribute anything, and we hope that against this background of common activity our theoretical position will assume its proper proportions for both sides, and that we shall be able to discuss it with no more spirit of controversy or systematised misunderstanding than Mr. Lloyd has shown.

(III, 1, 47–8)

The Detective Story

[January, February 1938]

Alick West

Some time before any detective stories existed (the earliest date from the last years of the eighteenth century), a new mood came into English literature which is an essential quality of the detective story – the mood of suspense.

Suspense

One sign of it is Samuel Richardson's abandonment of the 'I' form of the novel as used by Defoe in favour of a series of letters. As Richardson pointed out in the preface to *Clarissa Harlowe*, Defoe's technique precluded suspense. If the hero himself relates his adventures in the first person, the reader already knows he has come safely through them; if the novel is in the form of letters, he cannot know and is always on tenter-hooks. And according to Richardson's conception that could be the effect of the novel.

In poetry also the new mood can be felt against a contrasting boredom. Already in Pope, and stronger towards the middle of the eighteenth century, poetry became depressed with a general sense of weariness and futility. Young writes in his *Night Thoughts*:

> Live ever here, Lorenzo? – shocking thought!
> For what live ever here? – With labouring step
> To tread our former footsteps? ... to see what we have seen?
> Hear, till unheard, the same old slabber'd tale?

This depression alternates with bursts of intoxication, which 'whirl us (happy riddance) from ourselves,' as Young says in the same poem. The alternation between depths of boredom and heights of ecstasy introduces into poetry also the new quality of suspense: in his depression the poet is hoping for the rare moments of joy; and his joy has a desperate note, because he knows the boredom will return.

In the latter half of the eighteenth century this general mood of suspense finds one particular expression through the detective story. The first sign of a definite interest in detection (which was an old, but subsidiary, theme in literature) is a remark by Horace Walpole in a letter of 1754 that he had coined a new word – 'serendipity.' He explains that he had been reading a French novel entitled *The Voyage and Adventures of the Three Princes of Serendip*. When travelling in the East, the three princes are asked by a countryman if they have seen his camel. They have not, but they are able to describe it; it is blind in one eye, it has a tooth missing, and it limps. They have deduced this from observing that the bad grass on one side of the road was eaten, while the good grass on the other side was not, that gobbets of chewed grass the size of the gap left by a camel's tooth were lying on the ground, and that the prints in the dust were irregular. 'Serendipity' denoted such feats of deductive detection.

The suspense missing from these exercises of ingenuity (it is merely Sherlock Holmes deducing from Dr. Watson's stubble how the light falls when he is shaving, not Sherlock Holmes the sleuth) is present in Walpole's own work. His novel, *The Castle of Otranto*, written in 1764, may be termed the first thriller. It opens with the description of the preparations for the wedding of a nobleman's son. But the bridegroom is missing. A servant, with staring eyes, rushes in to the father, shouting 'The helmet! The helmet!' The son's mangled body is lying in the courtyard, crushed by an enormous helmet surmounted with a forest of sable plumes.

'The Novel of Terror'

Novels depending for their suspense on such mysterious incidents, with a background of murder, rape and torture, were highly popular by the end of the eighteenth century (they are often spoken of as 'the novel of terror').

Thus the suspense which had been growing since the earlier part of the century now centres round a mysterious crime.

There is, however, neither detection nor detective, only a succession of inexplicable happenings. But in many cases the author himself acts as a kind of detective, giving at the end of the book a rational explanation, supported by scientific footnotes, of the apparent mysteries.

One of the earliest and most notable novels where the detection of a crime forms the actual plot of the story was written by William Godwin, the author of *Political Justice*. The theme of his novel *Caleb Williams* (1794) is the discovery by the hero of a murder and his pursuit by the murderer.

Godwin writes in the preface:

> I formed a conception of a book of fictitious adventures that should in some way be distinguished by a very powerful interest. ... I bent myself to the conception of a series of adventures of flight and pursuit; the fugitive in perpetual apprehension of being overwhelmed with the worst calamities, and the pursuer, by his ingenuity and resources, keeping his victim in a state of the most fearful alarm.

He decided that the most impressive situation to account for the pursuit would be 'a secret murder, to the investigation of which the innocent victim should be impelled by an unconquerable spirit of curiosity.'

So the story runs. Caleb Williams begins to suspect that Frankland, by whom he is engaged as secretary, had committed a murder. His suspicion is confirmed. Frankland discovers that he knows, pursues him remorselessly, until Caleb Williams, reluctantly, denounces him.

To appreciate the quality of this story, it is necessary to remember the importance of suspense, mystery and crime in the best work of the period. They are very strong, for example, in Wordsworth, both in single passages, as when he describes how he rowed out on to a lake in a stolen boat and felt the mountain peaks pursuing him, and in his play *The Borderers*. Shelley wrote early novels of terror. There is the mysterious crime of Coleridge's *Ancient Mariner*, and the still stranger mystery of *Christabel*. The Byronic hero, filled with defiant remorse for some nameless deed, became proverbial. The early detective story is not a 'lower' kind of literature; it was one expression of a group of ideas and feelings which occupied the leading minds of the period. And this early detective story, *Caleb Williams*, is itself the work of such a mind.

Murderer Chases Detective

The significance of the crime and the criminal at this period
must also be observed. In the above-mentioned passage from
Wordsworth, the criminal is Wordsworth, stealing the boat and
challenging the mysterious power in the mountains. The old
man with the glittering eye in *The Rime of the Ancient Mariner*
speaks with Coleridge's voice. Byron's mysterious criminals are
himself idealised. Even if the idea and attitude represented by
the crime are finally rejected, the crime clearly has profound
and positive significance for the writer.

And *Caleb Williams*, being a part of the same general tendency, shows, not the detective pursuing the murderer, but the
murderer pursuing the detective. And when finally the detective, as a last resort, denounces the murderer to the law, he
despises himself for doing so; for Caleb Williams knows that
the murderer Frankland is a far greater man than he.

A similar attitude to crime is indicated by the fact that
during his flight Caleb Williams is welcomed kindly by the
head of a band of robbers, 'thieves without a licence,' as he
says, 'at open war with another set of men who are thieves
according to law.'

The general mood of suspense in the later eighteenth century thus finds expression in the novel of terror, in its particu-
larised form of the detective story, and in romantic poetry. In
each kind of writing the author and readers identify themselves
to a very considerable extent with the criminal and his crime,
although morality and law are finally invoked against him. The
early detective story shares in the confused revolutionary and
reactionary feeling of the romantic movement.

[Part 2]

After about 1820 the popularity of the novel of terror
declined. The supernatural mysteries of romantic castles no
longer thrilled. People's minds were too occupied with the
visible social issues. Alarmed by the workers' mass strikes
and organisation the bourgeoisie in 1829 set up their police
force. In the 'forties, as Thackeray wrote to his mother,
everybody was afraid of revolution and enrolling themselves
as special constables.

The bourgeois fear of revolution and their trust in the police resulted in the novel of terror becoming specialised in a new type of detective story. It cuts itself free from medievalism and becomes realistic. It leaves the Gothic castle for the town. It deals with contemporary life, and with crimes which are legally criminal, not morally wrong or metaphysically evil, as in the romantic movement. The criminal loses in intellectual and moral stature, and his crime in philosophical significance. The sympathy shifts largely from him to the detective. The detective is not the pursued, but the pursuer; and he hands over his prey to the police, not reluctantly, but triumphantly.

This change starts about 1840 with Poe (but the fierce contempt of his detective for the police still continues the romantic attitude), and proceeds through Wilkie Collins, *The Woman in White* (1860); A. K. Green, *The Leavenworth Case* (1878); to *The Adventures of Sherlock Holmes* (1893).

In these years the suspense connected with the crime and its detection has a different origin than in the romantic period. There is nothing revolutionary about it. The origin is rather in the suppressed fear of revolution. The suspense relieves, and the victory of the detective and the law reassures, this fear. The reader's pleasure comes through identifying himself with Sherlock Holmes, in highly respectable Baker Street, not with the common-place criminals (the clamour that Holmes should return after falling over the cliff with Moriarty was significant).

Since then a further change has taken place. The reader does not identify himself with the detective now as he did with Sherlock Holmes. This is owing to new methods of detection. 'Serendipity' is dead; the murderer can no longer be found by examining his hat. The characteristic method is mass investigation by the police – calling at all the houses in a particular district, circularising the textile and clothing industries to see where a thread was made, tracing telephone calls, etc. Deduction by the individual detective is only a part of this mass work.

Another reason why the reader no longer identifies himself with Inspector French, for example, as with Sherlock Holmes, is in the increased importance of chance – a man repairing telephone wires happens to look into the window of a room where the criminals think themselves unobserved, and his evidence gives a vital clue. In the measure in which the detective is assisted by luck, he means less to the reader than Sherlock Holmes; for his individual power is not so reassuring.

This element of chance, however, though it diminishes the individual detective, is not an unintentional weakness – at least not in the best work, such as that of Freeman Wills Crofts. For the tendency of the detective story to-day is to show through description of mass police investigation that any act – the crime – is embedded, as it were, in other acts; these other acts can be brought to light by a big organisation, thus giving a negative outline of the criminal act embedded in them. The interrelation between a crime and its environment are so intricate that no one can commit a crime and isolate it from its environment; at some point or other he makes a contact with social reality, which he forgets or cannot obliterate: he has to travel, buy things, telephone. And for the same reason the criminal cannot stage an act – an alibi, or a murder supposed to be suicide – without falsifying reality at some point. He either adds to or leaves something out of the environment surrounding his act: he forgets that a man who has hanged himself cannot get down to turn off the light. The apparent chance is thus really the certainty that the criminal cannot calculate all the chances; it is one aspect of the superiority of reality to all attempts to evade or counterfeit it.

Thus the basis of the good detective story to-day is the contact with social environment which the criminal inevitably makes. Sherlock Holmes had merely to look at the knees of a man's trousers.

The detective has become part of a state organisation; detection, mass investigation. The criminal has also changed. The reader having to be kept in suspense, the criminal is left as vague as all the other 'possibles.' If the author keeps his secret, there is no definite criminal till the end of the book; there is a general, abstract, potential criminality beneath respectable appearance. The substance of the detective story is the process by which the police materialise and arrest the abstract criminal by examining the indestructible social environment of his crime.

If the readers no longer have the same personal sympathy with the detective as with Sherlock Holmes, where do their sympathies lie in this struggle between police organisation and criminality? I do not think they are altogether on the side of the police. The reader is at least as much interested in the unknown criminal as in the police and their detectives, and he is more interested in the cleverness of the crime than of its detection. While the detectives become more and more uniform, distinguishable chiefly by their gags, the murderer becomes more and more ingenious. The kind of day-dream that occurs after finishing a detective story is not of oneself rivalling the detective – there's no use trying, for one can't even take a finger-print – but of oneself executing the perfect crime. The sympathy seems to be shifting once more back from the detective to the criminal (Edgar Wallace's *Four Just Men*, and Chesterton's *The Man Who Was Thursday* are significant; also the title 'The Crime Club,' not 'The Detective Club').

There is a similar change, I think, in the source of the feeling of suspense aroused. Partly, as in the period from Chartism till the end of the century, it derives from the fear of social upheaval; but the shift of interest to the crime and the criminal suggests that, similarly to the romantic situation, it springs not simply from the fear of social upheaval, but from a frustrated, contradictory, confused desire for it.

The social function of the detective story now is not so much to relieve and reassure, as in the middle period, as to divert a confused desire for social change into safe channels. It keeps it concerned with crime, and with a police force that has nothing to do but arrest murderers, never makes a baton charge, and always wins, because the very structure of society is its ally and the enemy of the criminal.

Ignoring the real function of the law and the police, and the real struggle against them, detective stories are finally dull, even though one cannot lay them down. The crimes are dull; they are merely the personal affairs of individuals who have to remain indistinguishable, and hence undistinguished. The police and detectives are dull, because they are not the police that matters. With the high lights of detection – for example, when Inspector French wakes up his wife with a shout, because he has got it – compare Caleb Williams' outburst:

> 'I exclaimed in a fit of uncontrollable enthusiasm, "This is the murderer; the Hawkinses were innocent! I am sure of it! I will pledge my life for it! It is out! It is discovered! Guilty upon my soul! ... I felt as if my animal system had undergone a total revolution. My blood boiled within me. I was conscious to a kind of rapture for which I could not account. ... In the very tempest and hurricane of the passions, I seemed to enjoy the most soul-ravishing calm.''

The solution, however ingenious, is unsatisfying, because it is no solution to that confused dissatisfaction with capitalist society which is one source of the interest in the crime. The detective story is a good example of that mediocrity which is the penalty for blinding oneself to what is vital in society.

That is the justification for the common criticism that the detective story reflects the decay of capitalism. But the significance of the shift of interest back to the criminal must also be kept in mind. Millions read the detective story, not because they are decaying with capitalism, but because they want to live and don't know how. The detective story is also a sign of revolt against decaying capitalism, while endeavouring to make that revolt harmless.

(III, 12: 707–10; III, 13: 795–8)

Plays about Trade Unionism[1]

[November 1934]

Barbara Nixon

Mr. Basil Dean has been known to say that all progressive play-producing societies both past and present, though they may have the best intentions to further the revolutionary movement, will begin and consequently end, by doing bad translations of foreign plays.

This, however, is not the place to discuss why there are so few plays which deal with working-class problems in this country, since *Six Men of Dorset* should be a notable exception precisely to this unfortunate rule. Here is a play placed in England, written in English and by an Englishman about the beginnings of the Trade Union movement in this country one hundred years ago – a movement of the highest significance, meaning life or starvation to millions of men and women. *Stevedore* is on the same subject, the struggle to-day to build up a union of black and white workers against the oppression of the Southern ruling class. The question of coloured labour is a local one, and the whole play takes place in America 3,000 miles away. But which has the more significance for the British worker? Without much doubt, the latter. The English play has neither the intensity nor the vividness of character of the American, there is far less urgency in the presentation of the conflict, and it has an atmosphere of remoteness greater than the lapse of merely a hundred years should warrant.

There are many points of similarity between the two. The Negro in America to-day is in many ways in the same position as the oppressed and frequently illiterate labourer of the early nineteenth century. In both plays there is the same necessity for a united and organized trade union; in both there is the same callous oppression, and the resort to illegal subterfuges to get a conviction on no matter what charge, so long as the *danger* of working class solidarity is avoided. But there is a difference between the two treatments of the problem as great as the difference in technique. Mr. Malleson's characters speak lines which are consciously important; frequently they have been taken from Loveless' diary. We cannot doubt the sincerity of the transcription, but at the same time it gives an impression of unreality, since few men speak to their wives or even to their parson in the language they use in a diary. The arguments have been made into dramatic dialogue, whereas in *Stevedore* there is real dialogue out of which the arguments emerge. Technically the Tolpuddle play is traditional; it uses the 'box-set,' and depends almost entirely for its emotional stimulus on the characterization of individual persons. It is a personal incident in a national and international problem. It is an epic theme; but the mode of treatment has limitations which preclude the emergence of an epic. History only acquires shape and significance when seen through the eyes of the present. Mr. Malleson has been content to observe from a distance: to show one isolated section of the picture, not as a symbol or an example of the whole, but cut out from its surroundings and remote from the present day. It is no defence to plead the hundred years which have elapsed. Tolpuddle cannot be remote when what those men fought for is still not accomplished, when large sections of the workers still remain unorganized, and the battle for the rights of speech and demonstration is assuming an increasing gravity to-day.

In the first two scenes Mr. Malleson gives us a vivid and moving picture of the destitution of the agricultural labourer, struggling to keep a family on 7s. a week; and again a mordant revelation of the perfidy of the farmers and the parson who agree to give a rise which in practice they fail to maintain. There is a good scene where the two delegates arrived from the London Grand National Consolidated Trades Union – Cobb, the more cautious, whose advice is to get what they ask for by legal means and at all costs to avoid force, and Brown, the younger man, who demands hotly why should they have to ask at all for what was originally taken from them. 'They're the *"Owners"* of all the land, and all that's on it! Who gave it to 'em? They took it! And there'll be no real justice, anywhere, till it belongs to all again ...' the trade union is 'a beginning. As long as, when we've got it we don't just go on asking ... they'll give us just as much as they have to – to keep us quiet; and no more. You said they were afraid. They are. But why?

Because they are not quite certain we know our place – underneath. And that means they don't feel quite so secure – on top. And that makes 'em savage.' Here indeed the play becomes very relevant to the present day; so much so that one questions whether it is not the actual voice of Mr. Bevin or Mr. Citrine, when Cobb asserts that 'this isn't a revolutionary country; and ours isn't a revolutionary movement.'

But despite these scenes and the admirable character of Betsy, there is something of that period air which haunts the more fusty of Shakespearian productions. It would be foolish to suggest that this is due to the extreme piety of George Loveless – so extreme that the character tends to become flat and unreal; this seems to be an historical fact, and Mr. Malleson could hardly portray him in any other way; and, indeed, the participation of the deity in the wage dispute certainly becomes less active as the play proceeds. It is not this, nor the idealized and whitewashed union members which creates the pervading atmosphere of remoteness, and at times of unreality. The play suffers because it is an over-faithful reproduction of the particular, and makes no attempt to reach the universal. This is true throughout, but abundantly so in the last scene, where, with one stroke, Mr. Malleson has sapped all the strength of the earlier parts. After the trial scene and the conviction, we see, not the efforts which resulted in a quarter of a million people presenting, successfully, a petition for pardon, not Loveless' homecoming, which might admittedly seem somewhat Utopian, not the struggle to build larger and more powerful unions, but the halcyon retirement in Canada of an old man and his family. In these last few pages Loveless tells the story of his deportation to his son-in-law. Even dramatically it is a lame conclusion, reminiscent of the Edwardian system of beginning a play with a discourse from the butler. When the recitation is over he says, 'I be tired ... now it's for them that come after.' This would be good if only we were given some slight faith in the power of these successors; actually we are given no signs even of their very existence.

If the play is produced again, and undoubtedly it should be, it is well worth seeing. There is a great deal that is both interesting and moving; it is only regrettable that the authors have not availed themselves of the vaster potentialities of such a theme. Perhaps more would have been possible had the play been required for a less august occasion than the Trade Union Congress. We are left with the impression that this was an era of calamitous mistakes and brutalities on the part of the ruling class, which would not occur to-day. Despite the personal victory of Loveless, there is a feeling of defeat – 'This incident is closed.'

In the last scene of *Stevedore*, on the other hand, Lonnie Thompson the Negro workers' leader, who almost alone has inspired them and led them to stand up for their rights, unlike Loveless, is killed, and for a moment his followers waver. But his death provides an immediate successor, and we know that the end of the play is only the beginning of a struggle which will be victorious in the end, however many leaders may be lost. The play is to be produced at the Embassy Theatre in November, and it should certainly be seen. The scenes in the Negro cook-shop and on the wharf are extraordinarily vivid, and the struggles of the white union leader and of Lonnie Thompson to overcome dislike on the one side, and distrust on the other, are economically and cogently shown; so also are the weapons of capitalism – organized hooliganism and lynch justice, and, most effective and international weapon of all, the splitting of the workers' ranks. Lonnie Thompson's urgent appeal is a message not only to the coloured workers of Southern America. 'Look at 'em, standing dar. De white boss spit in deir faces. De white boss make slaves out of dem – cheat 'em – rob 'em laugh at 'em. And dey just stands dar. "Beat me some mo', white boss. Sho', I like it. Beat me some mo'." Lawd, when de black man gwine stand up? When he gwine stand up proud like a man? ... We can't wait for de judgement day. We can't wait till we dead and gone. We got to fight fo' de right to live. Now – now – right now. We don't stand alone hyar. We ain't just a handful. Lem Morris' union, dey stand behind us too ... and dey gwine help us.'

Note

1. *Six Men of Dorset*, by Miles Malleson and H. Brooks (Victor Gollancz Ltd.); *Stevedore* by Paul Peters and George Sklar (Covici Friede, New York). Sklar is also co-author of *Peace on Earth*, an anti-war play which the Left Theatre is planning to produce this autumn.

(I, 2: 42–4)

Charlie Chaplin, 1936 [March 1936]
Elizabeth Coxhead

And so Charlie Chaplin has struck his first blow in the class-war. He has fluttered quite a number of dovecotes; he has got his film, supreme test of merit, banned in Germany. The left-wing audience may imagine from all this fuss that it will find in *Modern Times* a really stinging piece of social criticism. It will not.

Undoubtedly, Chaplin has been thinking, or rather feeling, a good deal about industrial conditions in America. It looks as though one should date his decision to make a film about them from René Clair's *A Nous la Liberté* – the influence of the ex-pupil on the master is too obvious to be accidental. The films begin and end alike, and the beginning of *Modern Times* is magnificent. A flock of sheep – then workers herded into the factory – then Charlie at work, endlessly twitching bolts on a conveyor. The boss orders a speed-up, the foreman speeds up, faster and faster Charlie twitches, until the terrible rhythm so dominates him that he can't stop twitching even during the lunch-hour, and rushes with his spanner at the buttons on people's trousers and anything else that looks like a bolt.

The boss decides to try out a mechanical feeder, which shall eliminate the lunch-hour altogether. Charlie is chosen for the experiment, and in one of the funniest sequences which has ever adorned a screen, he and the feeder meet, and the feeder wins. After that he is quite unnerved, and has to be rushed to hospital. They tell him to avoid excitement and worry, and turn him out penniless on to the world.

So far, you could hardly have a more biting satire on the system whereby machines devour men. But there, abruptly, it ends. The rest of his adventures are a series of unconnected episodes, invented just to raise a laugh, strung together without theme or climax. He has jobs, and he loses them, but it is no longer anything to do with the social system; it is because he

is inefficient, and the theme, if you can call it one, is a glorification of inefficiency. He is not even a real rebel. He gets
involved, but by mistake, in a demonstration of the unemployed, and is sent to prison; but he turns out to be on the
side of the warders, and protects them (more by luck than
good management, but still he does protect them) against a
prison riot, for which he is rewarded by a really cosy cell.

It would be fatuous to demand constructive propaganda,
from a film which only sets out to be a social satire; what one
does expect is that it should make the system it is satirizing
look ridiculous. Critics without a sense of humour attacked *A
Nous la Liberté* for not being 'constructive,' but it was fully
destructive, which was all that mattered. Its two tramps, when
they disappeared down the long road, had seen the triumph of
high finance swell till it burst like a bubble with its own
absurdity; they had been under-dogs and also bosses; they
knew the whole thing for a big fake. Charlie, disappearing
down the same road, knows nothing except how to run away
from the cops. It is he who is ridiculous; the cops and the law
and order they stand for, though rather disagreeable, seem to
be eminently sane.

Modern Times will shake the world, but only with laughter.
And that is more or less what the attentive student of Chaplin
and his methods would expect. His little tramp has always
been essentially sentimental, representing the pathos, and perhaps the dignity, of the under-dogs, but none of their more
practical and positive qualities; and he is therefore all wrong as
a central figure in a story designed to show up the absurdities
of the capitalists with whom he is contrasted. Nobody could
deny that Chaplin's heart is in the right place; he thinks
things are unfair and upside-down and wrong. But he has no
idea what is to be done about it. That is not his trade.

(II, 6: 274)

[Review of] D. H. Lawrence, *Phoenix*[1]

[January 1937]

Stephen Spender

This heavy, unattractive volume, a collection as it is of fragments and posthumous pieces, is nevertheless the most enliven-
ing book I have read for a long time, since a great deal of it is
D. H. Lawrence at his very best. Moreover, it is a panorama of
the whole Lawrence at every stage of his development: as a
young man, the son of a Nottingham miner, and the favourite
of his genteel and sensitive mother, against whose dominating
influence he was to strive long after her death; as a traveller,
restlessly going from continent to continent both to escape
from something and to discover a satisfactory way of life; as a
dying man, aware perhaps of the failure of his own quest and
yet still pouring out prophecy, an amazing analysis of contemporary middle-class society, and his gospel.

In one of these essays (on Galsworthy), Lawrence makes a few
remarks about literary criticism: 'Literary criticism can be no
more than a reasoned account of the feeling produced upon the
critic by the book he is criticising. Criticism can never be a
science: it is, in the first place, much too personal, and in the
second, it is concerned with values that science ignores. The
touchstone is emotion, not reason. We judge a work of art by its
effect on our sincere and vital emotion, and nothing else. ...

'Then it seems to me a good critic should give his readers a
few standards to go by. It is just as well to say: This and this
is the standard we judge by.'

I like this. Perhaps it would not apply for all the uses of
criticism, not, for example, for that which tries to 'dislodge' one
established poet in favour of another. But criticism which sets
out to create literary fashions, and then prove that the newest
fashion is unassailable, seems to me pretentious. In any case, one
cannot place a prophetic, intuitional and highly emotional writer

like Lawrence in such categories. One does judge him really by his effect on 'our sincere and vital emotion.' If he has none, he means nothing to the reader, that is all.

My standard in judging him is that I am a Socialist. Lawrence would probably not have accepted this; but then, in the last analysis, I do not believe he would have accepted any standard except his own. The penalty of being completely original is complete isolation; only Blake could really understand Blake, only Lawrence, Lawrence. The rest of us have to take from his work that which is useful to us, and reject what remains.

Lawrence's isolation and his desperate originality of thought were forced on to him by his social position. Born of a working-class family, he spent his life amongst the bourgeoisie, partly because intellectual life in England is predominantly bourgeois, partly because the sheer ugliness and hopelessness of the surroundings from which he emerged, depressed him. Yet he was acutely self-conscious socially, never fitted into any rank of society, and as a worker despised the bourgeoisie, whilst, at the same time, he could not bring himself to believe that the proletariat could offer any solution either for his or the world's problems. He did not fit into any social group or class. The solution which finally offered itself was sex; the meeting of two individuals, a man and a woman, became a substitute for his own lack of any fixed social background; so that an enormous amount of his work is devoted to invoking ways in which the sexual relationship may prove to be the means by which man shall rediscover his soul and his integrity. It is not too much to say that Lawrence saw sex as the pivotal point on which would turn a social revolution.

It is becoming rather fashionable to sneer at Lawrence's obsession with sex; yet it only became an obsession because sex did not take Lawrence far enough, so that at the end of his life he was left simply reiterating and insisting on the truth of his vision that the sexual relationship was wrong in contemporary society, and should be altered. I believe that Lawrence's pure intuition was quite right: the corruption of a society which sets commercial values above human values; which is at once cowed by fear of the body and sentimentalised by the duty of romantic love; which is either cynical or sentimental, portentous or flippant; all this is most evident in the relationship between men and women. I think Lawrence has gone further in describing, with the accuracy of genius, all the symptoms of a sexually neurotic society than Tolstoy, or even

than Freud, whose observations are necessarily confined to a
special class of pathological cases. What Lawrence saw very
clearly was that the bourgeoisie has really come secretly to hate
and trample on sex; idealised love and prostitution are only
two different ways of debasing the unpopular sexual act. He
saw, too, that older civilisations had a healthier and less inhuman attitude.

Whatever else Lawrence may be, he is first and last a revolutionary. Politically he was nothing, or, if you like it, anything.
For his opinions, when they are stated, are violently inconsistent
and can be fitted into several political philosophies. The Nazis,
with some justification, have claimed him as their own: for, when
his intuitions failed him, he gave way to mystifications about
Dark Forces, and even, in *The Plumed Serpent*, about Leadership.
But the difference between Lawrence and Nazi philosophy is that
the Nazi philosophy begins and ends with deliberate mystification; Lawrence only began to mystify himself when his intuition
did not lead him as far in solving the problem as he would have
liked. Strip away the mystification and one gets back to the
clearness and truth of his analysis of contemporary life.

Lawrence is a revolutionary because the only religion which
survives in bourgeois capitalist society, the only morality, is
respectability. And, as everyone knows, the clue to respectability is the middle-class attitude towards sex. It was against this
attitude that Lawrence led his devastating and courageous attack, not with satire, not with sentimentality, but by pointing
out that the accepted morality of our society had debased or
slobbered away the relationship of mutual respect for individual integrity, between men and women. His life task was to
make men and women desire a new and more vital relationship; if that were established, he believed that the motives
which have distorted and made inhuman the whole structure of
our society, would wither away. The emphasis he put on sex
may have been wrong. But no one can doubt its revolutionary
effect. I myself am only one of hundreds of young men who
have been first roused to an examination of the moral values of
capitalist society by reading Lawrence. His denunciation of one
institution at the very kernel of society was so true that it
radiated outwards, exposing all the other institutions in its
light. As Lawrence points out in his remarkable essay on
painting, at the end of a discussion of Cézanne's paintings of
apples, 'A new relationship between ourselves and the universe
means a new morality.' The reader of Lawrence discovers the

new relationship with the universe, and then he is involved in discovering for himself the implications of the new morality.

Lawrence hated politics because he saw them as forms of idealism, self-seeking materialism, egotism. In his own life he had abjured class, country, civilisation even, and tried to rediscover his lost social background in his relationship with one woman. Therefore he hated any movement that involved masses of men. The revolution was for him the revolution of the individual in himself, then of the man and woman in their relationship with each other, radiating outwards.

Here, again, we can hardly accept his teaching, even though we recognise the truth of his vision. Until their material conditions are altered, the vast majority of people are prevented by upbringing, environment, lack of opportunity and a hundred other causes from leading the kind of experimental life which made a change of heart possible to Lawrence himself.

Lawrence saw that human relationships were wrong, the standards of capitalist society false; he said change the relationships, abolish the standards, and then the evils of the social system will crumble away. 'When men become their decent selves again, then we can so easily arrange the material world. The arrangement will come, as it must come, spontaneously, not by previous ordering. Until such time, what is the good of talking about it? All discussion and idealising of the possession of property, whether individual or group or state possession, amounts now to no more than a fatal betrayal of the spontaneous self. All settlement of the property question must arise spontaneously out of the new impulse in man, to free himself from the extraneous load of possession, and walk naked and light.'

What he forgets here is that those who already, by their birth and condition, are freed of the 'extraneous load of possession' are in no position 'easily to arrange the material world,' nor even to 'become their decent selves again.' Lawrence refused to recognise this. If he went to Nottingham, the countryside 'plastered with slums' depressed him unutterably, and he came away again. He saw ugliness as an expression of man's soul; not as an expression of the soul of one class which conditioned the slavery of another.

In the remarkable essay on Democracy, from which I have quoted the remarks above, Lawrence comes into the open about Communism. 'The one principle that governs all the *isms* is the same: the principle of the idealised unit, the possessor of property. Man has his highest fulfilment as a possessor of property: so they all say, really. One half says that the uneducated, being the majority, should possess the property: the other half says that the educated, being the enlightened, should possess the property. There is no more to it. No need to write books about it.' There is, in fact, just this more to it: that Communists would abolish private property. If Lawrence had realised what this means, he might have seen that one of the implications of the propertyless society, is a new relationship between men and between the sexes. Since he did not, we can accept his premises about society, even though we do not agree with his conclusions. For the revolt of his genius against bourgeois society was complete.

Note

1.   *Phoenix*, by D. H. Lawrence. *Heinemann*: 12s. 6d.

(II, 16: 902–4)

[Review of] *Not I, but the Wind*.
By Frieda Lawrence

[April 1935]

Douglas Garman

Mrs. Lawrence has had a lot to put up with from her husband's biographers. Their private life has been reported with such variety of hysterical malice and she has so often been charged with lack of sympathy and understanding, that it is not surprising she should have attempted to clear up misconceptions by giving her own view of their relationship. Unfortunately the result is no more satisfactory than previous biographies. Her narrative is inconsequent and scrappy, the unpublished letters are of little interest and, though her account of Lawrence's intimate life is more reticent than those we have been accustomed to by some of his admirers, her portrait adds little to our knowledge of the man and nothing to our understanding of the writer.

'I did not want to write this book,' she says in the Foreword. 'I wanted to give Lawrence my silence'; and one can't help feeling she would have done better to stick to her first thoughts. For the fact is, far too much has already been written about Lawrence, the individual, with the result that his real significance is in danger of being overlaid by the extravagant claims put forward by devotees. Doubtless the responsibility for this is largely his own. Not only does he seem to have found it necessary in everyday life to surround himself with disciples, but in this work itself the voice of the teacher, even of the prophet, became latterly more and more insistent; so that however convinced one may be that his enduring value is as an artist, it is impossible to evaluate that without also taking into account his creed.

It is one of the faults of Mrs. Lawrence's book that she

reverses the order. Lawrence, the writer, scarcely appears: all her interest centres in his 'message,' primarily as it concerned herself, secondarily as it may concern the world. But since Lawrence himself failed to make his message convincing – failed, probably, to be convinced by it himself – it was impossible she should succeed.

The great value of Lawrence's work is that, almost from the start, he realized as clearly as anyone, and with a far finer intensity of passion than most, the baseness and hypocrisy of the superstructure of society; and it is his great distinction that he never allowed his disgust to take the defeated form of cynicism. He understood that if humanity was to retain its dignity and vitality it must undergo a violent and profound change, but his understanding always remained an instinctive one. He distrusted, sometimes self-consciously, the intellect and so was thrown back upon intuition and emotion; and it is they that give to all his best work its intensity and peculiar insight. He relied on them just as much for his interpretation of character as for the nervous sensibility of his descriptive writing. What counted for him was his immediate apprehension, whether of scenery or of a human relationship, and to that is due the spontaneity of his style and the vitality of his outlook. But it was this same quality and his rejection of any attempt at intellectual abstraction that led him in the last resort to his pseudo-mystical conception of sex and his acquisitive theorizing about the primitive life.

All his life, Lawrence was in flight – France, Italy, Ceylon, Australia and finally Mexico – trying to find a society free from the death-germ of decaying capitalism; and as Huxley says in the Introduction to the Letters, 'His search was as fruitless as his flight was ineffective. He could not escape either from his homesickness or his sense of responsibility; and he never found a society to which he could belong.' But as neither Huxley nor Lawrence realized, his real flight had begun earlier, when he first escaped from the intolerable conditions of working-class life.

After *Sons and Lovers* he seems to have closed his mind to that part of his experience, for when it recurs he treats it either contemptuously or snobbishly. But one cannot help feeling that had he not turned his back on it, his passionate hatred for the sham morality and makeshift values of contemporary life would have led him to a more positive and valuable outlook. The energy he expended in looking for an acceptable society he might have put into helping create one.

As it was he never saw profoundly enough into the causes of the modern sickness he so much detested to be able to discover an adequate remedy. He saw the secondary symptoms of the disease and described them admirably, but he could not prescribe for it. From this point of view he failed, and the flimsy efforts of his biographers to prove he succeeded only rob his failure of its impressiveness.

(I, 7: 286–7)

Music and Decay [December 1936]

Stephen Spender

[Review of] *Ulysses*, by James Joyce.

Ulysses, by James Joyce, is the furthest extension into realism
of a realistic tradition beginning with *Madame Bovary*. Beyond
this point, realism becomes incoherent: already in *Ulysses* itself
there are great hunks of incoherence. For realism has aims
different from reportage: reportage interprets and has its roots
in the newspaper 'story' which discovers a plot in life even
where there is none. James Joyce's realistic method does not
interpret life: it represents it as disinterestedly and with as
great truth as possible.

Flaubert took one woman's isolated life in the French provinces for his peculiarly detailed introspective study. Joyce takes
one day in the life of three chief characters: instead of taking the
long-extended stalk, he gives the broad, squat cross-section. In
this transverse, arrested day in the lives of these very few people
one sees *into* their minds rather than watches their development.
One sees also a cross-section of the whole of their environment;
the final impression left by *Ulysses* is certainly not Stephen, not
Marion Tweedy Bloom, not Bloom (her husband) even, though
he is the most striking figure in modern fiction – it is Dublin.

There is no story in *Ulysses*, there are only the stage properties of life which the people carry round with them as a fictitious world of fantasy and desire more real even than their
surroundings. Stephen is haunted by the ashen breath of his
mother 'beastly dead,' at whose death-bedside he refused to
pray. Marion Tweedy Bloom is surrounded with the memories
of all the men with whom she has ever slept or wanted to
sleep. The sensitive and illuminating point in Bloom's obscene
and inquisitive existence is his love for his dead son Rudy,
which he transfers to Stephen.

If there is nothing in *Ulysses* which one can call a story, there is a prodigious amount of arrangement. Firstly, there is the disconcerting parallel with the *Odyssey* which the title conveys. Several critics have worked out the parallels between the works of Homer and Joyce, but, personally, I have not found that these added much to my understanding or enjoyment of *Ulysses*. In writing a book which expresses the formlessness of life – punctuated only by birth, love and death – it was probably essential for Joyce to impose some quite arbitrary scheme on his material, which has only a hidden relation to the significance of his book. If, instead of using the *Odyssey*, he had worked out secret parallels with the New Testament, for example, his arrangement would doubtless have been different, but the total impression would have been the same.

What is far more important than the parallels with the *Odyssey* is the musical arrangement of *Ulysses*. I am convinced that Joyce must be obsessed with music, and that when he starts to write he draws on patterns of musical form far more easily than on past literature. Moreover, his sensibility is not visual at all; it is consistently aural, though sometimes the musical images are broken across by powerful sexual fantasies. In fact, I believe that the immense difference between *Ulysses* and all other literature is that its roots are in classical music. Music provides all the virtues and all the vices of Joyce's style. His greatest virtue is his mastery of themes and phrases which he is able to use as themes. To take only one example, there is a little joke early in the book about the word 'Up' being written on a postcard – up, up. This is one of hundreds of little phrases which are repeated with the effectiveness of genius throughout the book. Whenever the particular phrase occurs, it has the effect of a minute phrase in a symphony taken up first, say, by the violins and later by the trombones.

No doubt these particular technical tricks of musicians in repeating their phrases move us because at certain levels our consciousness is musical. Dreams, for instance, are symphonic in form rather than visual, even though we see them: for what we see is arranged with a musical rather than a pictorial kind of significance. Yet it is not only the phrase – or, rather, hundreds of such phrases – which Joyce uses in this masterly manner, it is also his characters who supply the main themes. In the first part of the book the theme of Stephen Daedalus is built up, just as Mozart builds up a theme for each of his characters in turn in the first act of *Figaro*: then there follows the Bloom theme. Finally, when both these are brought against each other in the central scene – the play scene – of the book, the effect is simply that of a bass wood-wind instrument (Bloom) playing against a violin.

But Joyce has borrowed far more than the use of thematic material from music. He arranges his book in the form of separate movements, each producing an entirely different effect. This is emphasised not only by what happens, but, even more, by punctuation and style. And the musical arrangement is not arbitrary in the sense that the Odysseus one is. For the total musical effect of the book is that of a most masterly series of variations on several complex but repetitive themes. Each variation on the Bloom theme or the Stephen theme – once Joyce has built these up in our consciousness – has the effect of plunging us deeper and deeper in the fate of these individuals and in the surrounding life of Dublin. James Joyce is a great composer who has chosen to write novels instead of symphonies.

Even the musical arrangement is used for the purpose of representing reality. For example, in the play scene which forms the centre and the great climax of the book the variations, like those great variations at the end of Brahms's Fourth Symphony, seem to swing back from the present into the remote past, the past history of Bloom leers at us in the Red Light district of Dublin. Yet this past is only a stage property of Bloom's present. Joyce, true to his realistic method, refuses completely to 'go back' – that most artificial trick of novelists. He presents the past in terms of the present, and in these terms it consists of phantasmagoria of drunkenness each of which has the symbolic significance of an image in a dream: otherwise it would not be remembered. For we only remember that which we either desire to remember or that which – through a sense of our guilt in the past – we are compelled to remember: and both these forms of memory are ghosts which continually haunt us in the present.

The world which Joyce's immense system of realism presents is one of dust and ashes. His book has no 'message,' it provides no comment except the immense central satire of all the standards of nineteenth-century middle-class liberal materialism as they have soaked through to Dublin. Stephen, the poet, is a thin, ineffective figure – far less successful than Bloom – the person standing for a life of disinterested artistic creation, yet who has turned against himself with mockery and hatred. It is the obscene Bloom, the lower middle-class unidealistic Jewish climber, who is most at home in this world, and who even stoops to pick Stephen up from the gutter.

There is anger certainly in *Ulysses*, but from what quarter does it blow? I think that the only system of values left is the perverted catholicism which exists in the minds of those who were born catholics and have renounced their religion. They do not believe in life either on this planet or after death: all they still believe in is hell and death. The world of *Ulysses*, representing a complete breakdown of moral standards, is Hell; death, non-existence, ashes, decay are the final realities. The most moving, the most coherent moment in *Ulysses*, the pivot on which the whole book turns, is the moment in the brothel, when everyone dances round and Stephen suddenly calls out 'Dance of death.' At that moment the image of his mother appears before his eyes:

'*Stephen's mother, emaciated, rises stark through the floor in leper grey with a wreath of faded orange blossoms and a torn bridal veil, her face worn and noseless, green with grave mould. Her hair is scant and lank. She fixes her blue-circled, hollow eye-sockets on Stephen and opens her toothless mouth uttering a silent word. A choir of virgins and confessors sing voicelessly.*'

(II, 15: 834–6)

[Review of] New Poetry

Calamiterror, by George Barker. *Faber & Faber:* 5s.
Poems, by Rex Warner. *Boriswood:* 5s.
The Disappearing Castle, by Charles Madge. *Faber & Faber:* 6s.
Spain, by W. H. Auden. *Faber & Faber:* 1s.
The Fifth Decad of Cantos, by Ezra Pound. *Faber & Faber:* 6s.

[July 1937]

Stephen Spender

George Barker is the least politically conscious of these poets, he has by now been told by most of the critics that he is too absorbed in the private crisis of his own personality, yet I find that his poems give me a far deeper sense of the confusion and frustration of European civilisation than do Charles Madge's quick-change muse, Rex Warner's severely willed political puritanism, or Ezra Pound's vast cocktail of old-world beauty and Douglas economics.

Rex Warner is serious, honest, observant, passionate (and an important prose writer, to judge from what I have seen of the *Wild Goose Chase*), but he does not seem to trust sufficiently either his own intuitions or his own perceiving eye: he has the schoolmaster's habit of hammering in his moral with prodigious anvil strokes. His poetry is unsatisfactory because, although it is competent and sincere, his verbal sense and technical skill do not conceal the fact that he is always shifting from a poetic meaning back to a prose meaning. There are good lines and sharp observation –

> 'What I watch most is moss
> or leaves in alleys of air,
> the rasping blade of grass,
> tiny berries on a huge moor.'

A few more verses like this, and then Rex Warner's social

conscience takes up the pen and we are told how 'What most moves my mind is torture of man by man':

> 'How love is made to lose,
> and those who are high hate;
> how truth is taught to please
> and freshness finds defeat.'

In this stanza, excellent as is the intention, there is a failure of imagination, because the poet instead of referring, as he does in the first stanza, to the world of his unique inner experience, is drawing on a world of text-books and economics which he endeavours to translate back into the language of his own authentic inner experience. The process of translation is not convincing, as, indeed, it never could be. The poet is committed to what he can really feel with his imagination, whether he likes it or not, and if the paths of imagination do not lead back to his social conscience there is nothing to be done about it.

Rex Warner's poetry suffers from the excess of the poet's conscious will. He never looks at a bird or a berry or cracks a joke without one feeling behind his lines the pressure of a conscience determined to draw a moral and exploit a meaning. Yet this willed quality has in poetry exactly the opposite effect from that which it has in political action: in disciplined political action, the will makes the individual merge his individuality in the purpose of the whole movement. In poetry the will emphasises the education and particular social background of the individual and makes it impossible for him to forget his own individuality; whereas without the exercise of the conscious will he would draw on sources of his consciousness which are communal and not individual.

No poetry could be more arrogantly individualist, more the product of a Public School and Oxford education, with holidays on the moors, than Rex Warner's. Because he puts his will before his imagination, he never succeeds in breaking down the barriers of a social class and special environment, as Auden has sometimes done. For example, where Auden's buffoonery is nonsense appreciable by anyone, Warner's humour is patronising and embarrassing:

> 'You who adore
> don't do it any more.
> Give it right up
> and don't be a pup.'

Yet one of these poems, 'Nile Fishermen,' is an extremely successful piece of Marxist writing, and many of the poems about birds will please those who like close observation.

Calamiterror is the very opposite of Warner's *Poems*, it draws no moral, preaches no sermons, and has the minimum of reference to external theory, statistics, or even to a coherent material reality. The whole poem, rather than being plotted and arranged, springs from one centre and has no development, it is a firework, not an organism. The experience at the centre of the fire is the death of the poet's child.

I cannot pretend that George Barker's attitude to politics and to Spain in particular (the Civil War puts in an appearance in the last two cantos), is correct or even constructive. But he is prodigiously and genuinely 'aware' of what is going on. It is a matter of far greater poetic significance that Irun has broken into George Barker's poetry than that Rex Warner has translated his political views into poems which, one cannot help thinking, would be better if confined to what he sees. If I read in the newspapers about an air raid in Valencia, I am oppressed by the weight of the actual and menacing which may seem to obtrude for a moment on my own environment: if I dream about an air raid in Valencia, I realise that this part of contemporary reality has become, as a symbol, part of my own mental environment, with a special significance which I cannot elude. The difference between politics in Warner's poetry and that of Barker is the difference between the air raid which for a moment interrupts the process of my inner world, with the weight of an unpleasant obligation, and the air raid which has broken right into the centre of my dream and become one of the symbols of my mental life – in fact, the air raid which I have poetically 'experienced.'

The obscurities, the formlessness, the redundancy, the occasional vagueness of Barker's poetry, are all due to his enormous ego-centricity as a writer. The situation of the poet in *Calamiterror* is described in his own words:

'The centre of the heart like a red tree
Shoots forth a hand pointing towards mirrors.
And when I look I see myself embroiled like
The Egyptian corpse in images of self.'

Occasionally the external world is so clamorous that it forces itself into the whirlpool of the poet's private world:

'Continually the women weeping in Irun's ruins
Call in distress with voices like swans;
I hear that cry which breaks the womb or room
Wherever I stand and forces me to go.'

George Barker's world is obsessed, over-sensitive, hysterical, and perhaps, in the last resource, too passive towards experience. Yet ego-centric as he is, he is not surrounded by the hard shell of a determined 'character' which seems to make it so difficult for Rex Warner to experience anything in the sense that it becomes part of himself and not just a deeply felt intellectual concept. 'Irun's ruins' would speak to Warner with the voice of conscience demanding the voice of protest: they become part of Barker's spiritual habitation, and therefore Barker is capable of development, because he is capable of imaginative experience to the degree to which it is only possible to the true poet, the degree by which an imagined experience modifies the poet's whole being.

Charles Madge is more talented than either Warner or Barker; he has none of Barker's deplorable lapses into meaninglessness, he is not over-rigid, like Warner. Yet his poems mean far less to me than the other two volumes, because Madge's talent appears to me to be exclusively directed towards enabling him to slide from one elusive mental position to another. Two things are symptomatic of this elusiveness: firstly, the unsimilarity of each poem in this book to any other (excepting the eight *Delusions*, here printed separately, which were originally one long poem); secondly, a steady falling-off in the interest of the poems (they are printed in the order in which they were written) as the book proceeds. The later poems are concerned far more with attitudes and effects and less with saying anything than the early ones. Charles Madge has extraordinary virtuosity; and his imitation of Gray's *Elegy* in *Delusions* is as masterly as it seems to me pointless. Perhaps I may misunderstand him completely, and in case I am doing so, I shall hasten to enumerate what seem to me his virtues. His achievement is a negation rather than an affirmation, and perhaps that is to the good: it is an astonishing impersonality. His poems have no rhetoric, they say little or nothing, they have a clear, exact imagery, a beautiful music, and they leave often the impression of something colourless and transparent. Technically, his poems seem to stand midway between the imagists and the surrealists. He very often succeeds in constructing an extremely successful 'word picture' with a poem. Possibly Madge has withdrawn his interest from writing poetry lately, in order to concentrate on other things. In any case, everyone seriously interested in Modern Poetry – especially in the writing of it – should read these poems. Technically it is of more importance than the other volumes.

Auden's *Spain* is an occasional poem in the same sense as are the poems by Wordsworth, Byron and Landor on the struggle of the Spanish people against Napoleon, and it is worthy of a great tradition. The poet has confined himself to an abstracted view of the fundamental motives of the struggle and a bird's-eye view of Spain:

> 'On that arid square, that fragment nipped off from hot
> Africa, soldered so crudely to inventive Europe;
> On that tableland scored by rivers,
> Our thoughts have bodies; the menacing shapes of our fever
> Are precise and alive.'

Within these limits, in which the element of personal experience and direct emotional response is rigorously excluded, the poem is a remarkable interpretation of the issues and implications of the struggle in Spain.

Ezra Pound goes on and on and on with his Cantos. If one imagined a person called Rabbi Ben Ezra £ writing an immense poem suggested by the antique flavour of his own first name plus the sense of a money civilisation suggested by the second – well, that poem might be very like the Cantos. In these Cantos, as in the early ones, there are passages of classical beauty inserted amongst great tracts of the Social Creditor looking at history and life. A certain dullness weaves together these divergent interests and ages into a sort of whole.

(III, 6: 358–61)

V.   Readers' Competitions

The readers' competitions make a fitting section with which to conclude the selections from *Left Review* because their changing status gives a subjective reflection of the magazine's evolution. A prominent feature of *Left Review*, especially in the first year, the competitions provided a democratic way of pursuing the objectives of bringing culture into the class struggle on the side of the working class and of promoting new writing. The assumption was that there were many readers who had much to say but who had no opportunity to put their thoughts and experience into writing and who, often without much education, probably lacked the confidence to write.

This was in no way sentimental; it was implicit in a social definition of literature. That is, literature is part of changing the world; it must therefore display an understanding of experience and also a motivating force. 'We seek to move our readers, to make them see what we see, to show them a world that seems to them inchoate in the focus of a definite and intricate pattern' (I, 1: 39). Art has a 'scientific' element, 'the fitting on to a particular section of the real world of a hypothesis'. Writer-readers can help test the hypothesis. And they can test the other vital aspect of the art work, its communicative capacity: the work of art 'is not complete until it has been received, i.e., not necessarily understood, not necessarily enjoyed, but either understood or enjoyed, or in some way has struck a spark from somebody else'. The poem or picture is different from the fantasy constructions of someone dreaming because they are meaningful 'both to the creator and to somebody else' (I, 1: 39, 40). It was assumed that reader-writers could have genuinely valuable insights; they were not condescended to.

However, not everyone agreed that readers' competitions had a revolutionary value. Professional expertise was considered by some to be what was needed, and popular participation and popular culture were judged to be of little value. This is in part the argument over the relative value of abstraction and concreteness that still dogs politics and cultural studies. Douglas Garman, consistent with his editorial role on *The Calendar of Modern Letters* some ten years earlier, insisted on the revolutionary primacy of an intellectual critique. Rather than encouraging creative writing by amateurs, *Left Review* should work 'to build up a structure of thought which will make truly revolutionary literature possible', he said in his contribution to the Writers' International Controversy (see Section I). He demanded 'precise and cogent meaning' and 'sound ideology', which criticism but not imaginative writing could deliver. The declining importance of the competitions parallels the growing reluctance in the later years of *Left Review* to explore people's experience, and the increasing reliance on 'authoritative' interpretation.

Topics for competitions included such things as a shift at work and a strike – which might well be expected – but also broader subjects, such as a description of a person and an imaginative reflection on how their character was formed. The editors offered a general critique of the entries in the competition report, which could be a guide for future contributions.

The way in which the first competition was introduced characterises fairly clearly the whole enterprise. Amabel Williams-Ellis, one of the editors of the magazine and herself a novelist, began with a narrative of four writers from different countries sitting round a table in New York discussing reasons for poor circulation of the workers' press. Apart from problems of hostile distributors, financial troubles and other material difficulties, it was concluded that jargon put off many potential readers. Amabel Williams-Ellis did not dismiss this merely as weakness on the part of writers but saw it as a genuine difficulty in dealing with new ideas. The focus was not on the writing for its own sake but on the *need* to deal with political issues: 'It may be difficult to write about modern politics in popular language, but it has got to be done. It is absolutely necessary' (I, 1: 39). The problem is seen as growing out of a practical situation and is presented embodied in experience; Williams-Ellis leads the reader from experience to generalisation, without mystification or demanding any conceptual leaps. Once the problem has been made clear, then the role of competitions is introduced:

> In order that we may learn by each other's attempts and each other's criticisms, I suggest that those readers who are also writers, but may

not, in some particulars, be satisfied with their technical skill, should
join us here in discussion and in attempting practical solutions. To
that end a series of exercises or competitions would, it seems to me,
be useful. (I, 1: 40)

Williams-Ellis gives an extract of some 700 words from her
own novel *To Tell the Truth*, depicting an eviction. What entrants are asked to do is to 'describe the same scene from
another point of view ... the camera can be shifted to any other
angle that the competitor fancies' (I, 1: 40).

The first selection printed below is the report of this competition, which appeared two issues after the competition was
set. It is detailed and offers constructive criticism, and it is in
this context that the next competition is introduced. There are
also accompanying suggestions that should be helpful to writers
faced with trying to explain a scene they are themselves very
familiar with for the benefit of readers who may need to have
the details spelled out in order for it to make emotional sense.

The second selection is Amabel Williams-Ellis's setting in
issue no. 7 of the third competition. It follows the pattern
suggested in the report of the first competition, a general
topic given particularity by the writer, but it emphasises
further that particularity is to be taken seriously because, as
her brief illustrations show, any reality has a great complexity of determinants. The view of literature presented goes
well beyond mere recognition of individuality; it insists on
its fundamental importance. Reality here is multi-faceted and
is composed so much of unique elements that, even though
social types can be recognised, it cannot easily be made to
conform to a line. She had already emphasised the importance of sense experience and concrete detail in setting the
second competition in December 1934:

Once more the reader should be made to use at least four of his five
senses. He must *feel* the smoothness of the tools, the heat or coldness
of what is touched, *hear* the clatter of pots and pans, or the much
more rhythmic beat of machinery, or if the worker is an errand boy,
the sounds of traffic in the streets, the calls across the street of boy to
boy, or if the worker is a miner, the strange, peculiar muffled clanks
and deep-toned clatters of a mine. Then there is the *smell* of warm oil
on a machine, or of cooking or washing, or earth turned up by the
plough. Every job has *smells*, *sounds* and sensations of *touch* besides
heat and cold that will help to make it real to the reader. (I, 3: 74)

After the first year the competition setters already seemed to be losing faith in art's potential. The competition of October 1936, two years on, had 'What Life Means to Me' as the theme, but it was an essay that was demanded, not fiction. The material for the essay was seen as generalised experience rather than significant concrete detail:

> Your essay should be built around your family and emotional life; your age; your job, its conditions and wages or salary; your recreations and hobbies; the organisations, political or cultural, in which you are active; your prospects for the future and general attitude to the world. (II, 13: 680)

Amabel Williams-Ellis had shown a large-spirited trust in the competitors to judge for themselves what was significant; that trust seemed to be disappearing from *Left Review*. The winning entry of the competition 'On Taking Politics Seriously', announced in the January 1938 number, had interesting experience but lacked imaginative or literary qualities. It is the surface content, line, that is considered important; there is no place for nuance or qualitative variation.

The last competition reprinted here is one on criticism. Williams-Ellis's voice can still be heard in it, but she has not been allowed to sing her own tune; there is more demand for *explicit* message than she found useful. The direction to the would-be critic to examine the two stories for 'a correct attitude towards strikes' suggests a reductive vision of literature. It also suggests that Douglas Garman's preference for a professional approach to literature, relying on experts, was taking precedence over the democratic attitudes that Williams-Ellis found basic to meaningful literary discussion.

Our Readers Get to Work

[December 1934]

Amabel Williams-Ellis

A number of workers have entered the competition which was set in the first number of *Left Review*. Readers will recall that a sample was given of a street scene, from a novel by the present writer ("To Tell the Truth"). The scene was an eviction and in the sample was seen through the eyes of a bewildered onlooker. It was suggested that competitors should 'shift the camera' and show the same or a similar scene through the eyes of one of the other participants.

George Evans from Glamorgan chose those of a miner.

'Dai coming back from the pit with his block of firewood tucked under his arm, clumped along, making the pavement ring with his nailed boots.'

A slack time at the pit has given Dai an unusual amount of time for thinking, an activity to which he is not accustomed as is his brother.

'Dai had a great respect for his brother, Evan. Evan while quite young had been compelled to relinquish work at the pit. He had been stricken with the miner's curse, silicosis.'

Evan had in fact given Dai the Marxist analysis of what was wrong with the world, and Dai, not having had Evan's time for study, was bewildered by it. As Dai thus walks along, he sees how 'in the doorway of No. 10 a tall dresser is in process of being removed from the house by two officious looking men, who, one at each end, are attempting to manoeuvre it through the doorway.'

The scene of the eviction is then given very much as before in the sample, Dai taking a leading part in trying to prevent it, and the struggle, in which Dai trips up the bailiff's man to the amusement and delight of the crowd, is quite well described. The scene ends, as in the sample, with the arrival of the police.

187

'Put on your skates, Davy, here's the cops!' Dai escapes, his last act being to drop his block of firewood on the bailiff's toes; the boy reaches one more stage in his conviction of the truth in his brother's statements.

I hope the author of this entry will continue to try his hand at writing, and more especially that he will watch out for the sights and sounds of what he knows to be going on. It is the job of a writer to convey as sharp an impression of what is described as possible, and George Evans has several little touches, which definitely make the reader use his ears, as he should. The reader should, when reading a description generally be made to use at least four out of his five senses, smell, hearing, taste, sight and touch.

Another contribution comes from Sheppey, in Kent. F. C. H. Whitehead says in his letter that he thinks that constructive criticism, such as the *Left Review* offers, 'should go a long way to assist us to evolve a literature which, though revolutionary in content, does not make too big a break with the bourgeois forms of expression which, in this country, are the only standards of criticism and approach.'

(He had previously given reasons why he thought that the German and Russian revolutionary tales were not necessarily helpful examples for us here.) He tells *Left Review* to go on, and help workers 'to create a real workers' literature from the workers' point of view.'

This competitor sees the eviction through the eyes of Harry the bailiff.

'Being a bailiff had its disadvantages in the Green Street quarter. You was fair game for all the kids what wanted a lark and you daren't 'it 'em for fear of what you'd cop....' This bailiff admired finesse:

'Alf,' said he to his newest, and least known assistant, 'go round to 'Ubbles in Green Street where I puts in the order, knock at the door, all innocent as if your 'oop's fallen down the grating (Alf forced a grin, Harry was a wit) and stand there as if butter wouldn't melt in your mouth, and me and 'im (indicating George, the other assistant) will do the trick.'

Alf goes and knocks, the other two bailiffs wait in a pub opposite the house. The child (as in the original sample) thinking that the knock is his mother's (back from shopping,) opens the door and immediately Alf and the two waiting bailiffs make a rush.

'The swing doors still swung and the front door slammed,

they had been more successful than they had imagined possible.' They begin to put out the furniture. 'Slowly, and with painful effort, they began to twist and manoeuvre the sofa through the passage, its legs with the jingling castors scraping the damp, be-flowered walls, leaving gashes and weals in its wake.'

Opening the door they find a knot of neighbours gathered, which is slowly augmented as more and more of the inhabitants of the street realize what is going on. Some spirited dialogue follows.

The owners of the house come home, first the mother, with her baby in her arms, and the boy who has unwittingly let this misfortune fall upon the family realizes what he has done.

'Mrs. Hubble cast her eyes round anxiously for her boy. He returned her look and with a howl buried his face in her rusty skirt. No reproach or protest came from Mrs. Hubble, a quiet, crushed young woman, worn out with the struggle of continual unemployment.'

The bailiffs redouble their efforts and admonish the crowd that 'they ought to know better than to resist the law.' As in the original, the owner of the house returns on the run, and in the scrimmage, the sofa is forced back into the house. The bailiffs send for the police.

'Dirty 'ole as this is,' returned Hubble, 'It's better than the 'Ouse, which is where I ain't going while can 'ang on 'ere.'

The arrival of the police scatters the crowd, but the Hubbles are back in their house and have barricaded it, and they are left standing siege.

The fault in this, as indeed in most of the entries, is that it seems to the present writer that the sample has been too closely followed and the competitor has not given himself enough rope. This contribution as a whole shows that this writer has a sense of dialogue and knows how excited people talk. Might I hope that he too will enter for the next competition and suggest that, as dialogue seems to be a tool he uses well, that he tries to make his next entry consist as much as possible (as a play does) of the words of the actors.

'Tom A. Mac.', writing from Liverpool, also has a suggestion to make in the note with which he accompanies his entry.

'I am not a writer but a reader of your magazine. I wish there were more like it, and could they be made available to we unemployed workers through a Workers' library, and loaned out at a cost of 1d. or 2d. In this city, there is no decent Workers' Library.'

This seems to the editors of the *Left Review* an excellent and practical suggestion. Perhaps this competitor would try to organize a Reading Circle – *Left Review* would willingly co-operate? Other readers might perhaps send suggestions as to the best way of organizing this. Such circles would add great value to *Left Review*.

'Tom A. Mac.'s' entry has followed the original sample rather too closely – he has in fact altered it almost solely in making it shorter and making the character who is the on-looker in the sample into an active participant who helps to get the furniture back into the house.

The Prize goes to N. N. D.   after some debate between its merits and those of F. C. H.   Whitehead's entry. This competitor has seen the scene through the eyes of a young police constable, who is summoned to the aid of the bailiffs, and begins as follows: –

'Eviction,' said the sergeant, 'two of you will do.' P.C. Jones and another left the station and made for the scene of the eviction. ...

'21 Geranium Road, he knew the place pretty well, a row of low, ancient, tumble-down cottages, the iron railings in front of most of them were broken, panes of glass in the windows broken and replaced with brown paper, ragged curtains at the windows doing their utmost to hide the soap box furniture within.'

But on this afternoon a crowd of people, who are not the people of Geranium Road as he knows them, are listening to a speech that someone is making to them from an upstairs window.

'Down Geranium Road nobody ever got drunk, he could walk down there on a winter evening and hardly a light would be seen in any of the houses, hardly a sound, just perhaps the fretful crying of some discontented baby. ...

'He knew the curious crowds that collected at the scene of an accident, his "Move along there," "Now then what's all this about" rose to his lips and died in quick succession. The occasion was all wrong, this was not a curious crowd at an accident, it was a crowd with a purpose, he felt the purpose. He elbowed his way through, there were mutterings from the men, the women were more vociferous. A man in a bowler hat rose from his seat on the broken-down railings. 'Ah, now we'll see,' he said. He was the bailiff's man. A bucket of water sloshed down onto his coat, P.C. Jones stepped back hurriedly, he felt amused, he didn't like the look of the bailiff's man....

'A bit of a struggle was going on in the kitchen. The bailiff's man held two legs of an old table, the man who had been speaking from the window held the other two legs. They were pulling each against the other, a crack and the table parted. A look of triumph on the face of the bailiff's man, a look of dismay and then of hatred on the face of the other, and he flung the broken part at the bailiff's man.'

Next day it is P.C. Jones's duty to testify against the tenant of the house.

'As he described the scene to the magistrates, he remembered the dismay on the man's face as his rickety old table had cracked and broken. Now as he looked at the prisoner, he saw nothing but hate. When he saw the table crack, he too felt pity for him and hatred for the bailiff's man, so triumphant. It was that pitiful look of dismay that had aroused his own pity. Now, when he caught the defiant hate on the man's face, he felt no pity, he could not describe his feelings at all. He felt neither pity nor hate, it was a new feeling to him, something like sympathy, only stronger.' Perhaps the reason why the treatment here is fresher is found in a little note which is appended to it. 'I have mislaid my copy of *Left Review* and forgotten the conditions.' Perhaps it is because she had not the sample description by her, and she has not followed it so closely as most of the other competitors, that 'N. N. D.' has realized a real road, and has drawn the scene quickly. The phrase 'discontented baby,' is excellent. The slightly unexpected but correct word makes the reader use his ears directly.

Will 'N. N. D.' note that her prize is a book up to the value of 10s. 6d. to be ordered from any bookseller advertising in *Left Review*. She should write to the editors saying what book she wants; she wrote her name and address in pencil and the editors have grave doubts about it!

Since contributors show signs of following a sample rather closely the subject of the next competition will be given without one. The subject is *either an hour or a shift at work*. The idea this time being merely to produce a picture, not a painting but a 'sound' picture in the cinema sense. The 'shift' at work described could be either the time spent by a housewife between getting the children off to school and their coming back to dinner, or the same housewife doing shopping or bathing the children or if the competitor lays the scene at a works it might be the time between clocking in in the morning and the dinner hour, or the dinner hour and time to knock off. He or she might be a printer, a textile worker or in a shop.

Another scene which would have great possibilities would be men at work on a building job. If the competitor wants to go in for detail an hour would be long enough. Once more the reader should be made to use at least four of his five senses. He must *feel* the smoothness of the tools, the heat or coldness of what is touched, *hear* the clatter of pots and pans, or the much more rhythmic beat of machinery, or if the worker is an errand boy, the sounds of traffic in the streets, the calls across the street of boy to boy, or if the worker is a miner, the strange, peculiar muffled clanks and deep-toned clatters of a mine. Then there is the *smell* of warm oil on a machine, or of cooking or washing, or earth turned up by the plough. Every job has *smells*, *sounds* and sensations of *touch* besides heat and cold that will help to make it real to the reader. Remember that is the heart of this whole business to make the reader feel as if he or she were actually there. Remember it is the unexpected but correct word that does the trick.

This time, the writers should draw no moral, but merely paint a scene. It can be supposed to be part of a longer story or of a novel, in which the writer is supposed to have the opportunity to draw his or her conclusions.

(I, 3: 71–4)

Competition [April 1935]
Amabel Williams-Ellis

The subject for the next *Left Review* Competition is 'An Encounter.'

The writer meets someone – perhaps he only passes him in the street. Perhaps he meets him in the course of a talk at a pub, at work, or at home. Anyhow, the writer gets a strong impression of this man or this woman and begins to think of all the big and little things that have made him, or her, that person and no other. That other person was once a child: went to school (was shy or bold, clever or stupid, happy or unhappy). Then that queer time 'the teens' when we nearly all believe that almost anything might happen, that we might turn into almost any sort of person – a film star, an explorer, keep a chemist's shop, drive the biggest engine of all, pilot an aeroplane, breed *the* whippet, or *the* carrier pigeon or marry the young man with the long eyelashes.

What became of all those funny dreams – many of them a lot queerer than that? How did life really turn out for this one? There was, the writer may be sure, work – or perhaps its horrid counterpart a vain search for work; some sort of love affair; lots of worry, some fun we hope. All these things formed the person that the writer is looking at. Did this man or woman think about everything as it came along, ponder and turn it over: or just live and let things happen?

The writer can trace a history by all the little signs; dress, attitude and so on, (a miner doesn't walk, sit, or dress like a tailor, nor a publican's wife like a school mistress, nor she like a shop assistant, nor she like a textile worker) or get the whole impression from what is actually said. That whole impression can sum up a long life or be the hopes and fears of a young person or a child looking forward: can tell of an oddity, or of a person who looks and thinks like a rubber stamp. But the person, the talk, or the scene, has got to be strongly brought before the reader in about a thousand words.

Your sitter is waiting for you, – opposite you in the train, perhaps at home, by your side at work, or on the other side of the counter. Give us a thousand words of vivid portraiture.

Many people are interested and are watching our competitions. A well-known publisher has written to one of those whose entry was published in the last issue. The work of competitors is being regularly read and enjoyed, to the editor's personal knowledge, by four or five well known novelists and writers, and best of all the editors have received extremely encouraging letters from the competitors.

'It was revealing to see my entry among the others.' The criticisms offered were also apparently found helpful. 'By precept and example LEFT REVIEW does well what no other Journal does at all' says one of our competitor correspondents. 'I swelled so much with pride that I burst two waistcoat buttons,' says another.

The editors hope and believe that *Left Review* can help in building up something new in the literature of this country but they can only do it with the help of the workers.

We hope that novices will realise that it is well worth while going in for the competition. Several of those whose work attracted attention last time had never written before.

(I, 7: 277)

Competition in Criticism [October 1935]

The subject for the next *Left Review* competition is: A Criticism of the two stories printed above.

Entries, which should be short (not more than one page of typescript or two of handwriting) should be sent to Sylvia Townsend Warner, 24 West Chaldon, Dorchester, Dorset, before November 1st, 1935.

The standard of judgment is clear. As Dimitrov said: 'Literature must serve the great revolutionary ideal of millions of workers.' It is in the application that questions arise.

One standpoint says that criticism should consider primarily the content. In terms of the subject of this competition: Examine whether the sketch expresses and tends to encourage a correct attitude towards strikes. The other standpoint says: Examine whether a vivid impression of the scene is conveyed, irrespective of content, and by what means.

We do not believe that either kind of criticism is adequate by itself. The first is the same thing in criticism as Dimitrov attacked in literature when he said: 'The man who limits himself to repeating "Long live the Revolution" is no revolutionary writer.' The man who places a work according to its manifest revolutionary content, leaves the real work of criticism untouched. For the particular way in which the content is expressed – in the case of a short story or sketch, the construction, the movement, the drawing of the characters, the dialogue, the style – is an essential part of the content, just as the tone of a man's voice is an essential part of what he says, and often more expressive of what he means than his words – which it may contradict. Good criticism must always render the tone of a writer's words and its significance, the way in which it modifies and possibly contradicts the manifest content.

On the other hand, discussion only of style, construction, movement is wrong, because there is no movement in the abstract. However expressive the tones of a voice, they are only expressive because this particular thing is said with this particular intonation and rhythm. Unless the form of a story is discussed in relation to the content, we are discussing literature apart from its practical intention in actual life; and that practical intention is the final essence of everything we say, however abstract the form.

Criticism must examine not only the content, but also the particular way in which the content is expressed; it must examine the form, not in terms of abstract ideals of form, but in relation to the practical social significance of what is said in that form.

We would particularly ask competitors to bear in mind that the first condition of good criticism is complete frankness in stating their impressions, especially those impressions which at the first taste seem indefinable. Secondly, the relation between critic and literature is not one between an unconcerned observer and his object. The critic must actively relive the writer's experience as his own, and then criticize the involuntary comments he has made to himself during that experience, applying to himself the same standards as to the work to be criticized: Do I like this because it expresses what I believe in, or only because it gratifies the reactionary habits of thought I am fighting against?

(II, 1: 32–3)

Notes on *Left Review* Authors

Blumenfeld, Simon: a clothing worker who became a novelist; *Jew Boy*, 1935; *Phineas Kahn: Portrait of an Immigrant*, 1937.

Blunt, Anthony (1907–83): *Artistic Theory in Italy*, 1940; *Art and Architecture in France, 1500–1700*, 1953; *The Art of William Blake*, 1959; *Nicholas Poussin, 1594–1665*, 1965; various books on drawings in the collection of Her Majesty the Queen at Windsor Castle.

Brown, Alec: poet and novelist; translated from Russian, French and German; *Daughters of Albion*, 1935; *The Fate of the Middle Classes*, 1936.

Calder Marshall, Arthur (1908–92): novelist and essayist; *Pie in the Sky*, 1937.

Cunard, Nancy (1896–1965): poet; edited *Negro* (1934).

Day Lewis, Cecil (1904–72): poet and writer on poetry; translated Virgil.

Fox, Ralph Winston (1900–36): novelist and political historian; biography of Lenin, 1933; translated Plekhanov's *Essays in the History of Materialism*, 1934; *Captain Youth: A Romantic Comedy for All Socialist Children*, 1922; *The Novel and the People*, 1937.

Garman, Douglas (1894–1969): poet; translated from French; founder and editor of *The Calendar of Modern Letters*; secretary to the Editorial Council of *Modern Quarterly*.

Gill, Eric (1882–1940): sculptor, engraver, typographer; *Christianity in the Machine Age* (1940).

Grassic Gibbon, Lewis (1901–35): pen name of James Leslie Mitchell; *A Scots Quair*, 1932–34.

Holtby, Winifred (1898–1935): novelist; *South Riding*.

Jackson, Thomas Alfred (1880–1955): *Dialectics: The Logic of Marxism and Its Critics – an Essay in Exploration*, 1936; *Charles Dickens: The Progress of a Radical*, 1937; *Ireland Her Own: An Outline History of the Irish Struggle for National Freedom and Independence*, 1946.

Jellinek, Frank: *The Paris Commune of 1871*, 1937; *The Civil War in Spain*, 1938; various translations.

Lehmann, John (1907–87): poet; *New Writing*, 1936.

Lindsay, Jack (1900–1990): numerous books on art, literature and history.

Lloyd, Albert Lancaster (1908–82): folklorist and musicologist; translator; sometime whaler and sheepherder.

MacDiarmid, Hugh (1892–1978): poet; 'First Hymn to Lenin'; defender of Scottish culture.

Madge, Charles (1912–1996): one of the founders of Mass Observation; poet.

Morton, Arthur Leslie (1903–87): historian, poet; *A People's History of England*, 1938.

Nixon, Barbara: actress, active in left theatre.

Read, Herbert (1893–1968): poet, wrote on poetry and art.

Rickword, Edgell (1898–1982): poet, translator, critic; *Scrutinies by Various Writers*, 1918; edited *The Calendar of Modern Letters*, 1925–27.

Slater, Montagu (1902–64): novelist, playwright; *The Second City*, 1931; *Easter 1916, Stay Down Miner*; libretto for Benjamin Britten's *Peter Grimes*.

Spender, Stephen (1909–95): poet; memoirs of 1930s.

Strachey, John (1901–63): numerous books on politics and economics.

Swingler, Randall (1909–67): poet and novelist; literary editor of *Daily Worker*; choral collaboration with Alan Bush.

Townsend Warner, Sylvia (1893–1978): novelist; *Lolly Willowes*, 1926.

Van Gyseghem, André (1906–): theatre producer; *Theatre in Soviet Russia*, 1943.

Warner, Rex (1905–86): literature and mythology/anthropology; *The Wild Goose Chase*, 1937.

West, Alick (1895–1972): *Crisis and Criticism*, 1935; *A Good Man Fallen Among Fabians*, 1950.

Williams-Ellis, Amabel (née Strachey) (1894–1984): novelist and children's author and writer on science for children; *To Tell the Truth*, 1933; *The Big Firm*, 1938.

Wintringham, Thomas Henry (1898–1949): sometime member of Inner Temple 'disbarred for sedition and incitement to mutiny'; *Mutiny: Being a Survey of Mutinies from Spartacus to Invergordon*, 1936; *English Captain* (reminiscences of International Brigades), 1939; books on military subjects (e.g., *How to Reform the Army*, 1939).

Suggestions for Further Reading

Branson, Noreen. *History of the Communist Party of Great Britain: 1927–1941* (London: Lawrence & Wishart, 1985).

Bukharin, N. I. et al. *Problems of Soviet Literature*, ed. H. G. Scott (London: Martin Lawrence, 1935).

Caudwell, Christopher. *Illusion and Reality: A Study of the Sources of Poetry* (London: Macmillan, 1937).

——. *The Concept of Freedom* (London: Lawrence & Wishart, 1965). Contains selections from *Studies in a Dying Culture* (1938) and *Further Studies in a Dying Culture* (1949).

Clark, Jon, Margot Heinemann, David Margolies and Carole Snee. *Culture and Crisis in Britain in the Thirties* (London: Lawrence & Wishart, 1979).

Croft, Andy. *Red Letter Days: British Fiction in the 1930s* (London: Lawrence & Wishart, 1990).

Day Lewis, C. *The Mind in Chains: Socialism and the Cultural Revolution* (London: Frederick Muller, 1937).

Fox, Ralph. *The Novel and the People* (London: Lawrence & Wishart, 1937). Paperback reprint, edited and introduced by Jeremy Hawthorn (London: Lawrence & Wishart, 1979).

Fyrth, Jim, ed. *Britain, Fascism and the Popular Front* (London: Lawrence & Wishart, 1985). See esp. Margot Heinemann, 'The People's Front and the Intellectuals'.

——. *The Signal Was Spain: The Spanish Aid Movement in Britain, 1936–39* (London: Lawrence & Wishart, 1986). See esp. part 1.

Heinemann, Margot and Noreen Branson. *Britain in the 1930s* (London: Weidenfeld and Nicolson, 1971).

Hobsbawm, Eric. 'The Historians Group of the Communist Party' in *Rebels and Their Causes: Essays in Honour of A. L. Morton*, ed. Maurice Cornforth (London: Lawrence & Wishart, 1978).

Lewis, John. *The Left Book Club: An Historical Record* (London: Victor Gollancz, 1970).

199

Lucas, John, ed. *The 1930s: A Challenge to Orthodoxy* (Hassocks: Harvester Press, 1978).

Morton, A. L. *A People's History of England* (London: Victor Gollancz/Left Book Club, 1938).

Mulhern, Francis. *The Moment of 'Scrutiny'* (London: New Left Books, 1979).

West, Alick. *Crisis and Criticism* (London: Lawrence & Wishart, 1937). Reprinted in *Crisis and Criticism and Selected Literary Essays* (London: Lawrence & Wishart, 1975).

Index